U2

EXPERIENCE

CONTENTS

ABOVE: U2's bass player Adam Clayton during a performance on the 360° tour in 2009. When discussing the longevity of U2 he explains, "We won't let each other fail."

OPPOSITE: U2 playing to a hometown crowd at Croke Park, Dublin, in 1987 on the Joshua Tree tour.

INTRODUCTION

If you were to present a screenplay based on U2's career to a film studio, it would end up in the bin, dismissed for being far-fetched and completely implausible.

U2's truth is stranger than fiction: four teenagers still learning to play their instruments, three of whom are welded to a Christian prayer group that disapproves of the rock 'n' roll lifestyle, end up conquering the music world and remaining at the very top for over 30 years. Theirs is a music world story that has never happened before, and will most likely never happen again.

Next year (2016) it will be 40 years since Bono, The Edge and Adam Clayton crammed themselves into Larry Mullen's kitchen to audition for the band. There really wasn't anything there at the time except blind faith and determination. The fact that it took them four years to secure a record deal speaks of how musically unprepared they were. And just how unlikely they were as contenders for music's top table.

There were times when they were broke and disillusioned and very close to packing it all in. Theirs was a slow build – each successive album selling steadily more and their appeal very much rooted in the passion of their live performances. "U2 Could Happen to Anyone" was one of their early graffiti slogans. It was their mission statement.

From car parks to pubs to theatres to arenas to stadia, the live show was their weapon – part evangelical gathering, part musical maelstrom. Winning over hearts and minds was their agenda. And they would not be denied.

If ever there was some mythical rock 'n' roll rulebook, U2 never read it. Although forged in the white heat of the punk/New Wave musical era, they never subscribed to its pieties. They wanted the big stage. Bono felt he had something to say; The Edge, Larry and Adam knew how to give that message a musical expression.

Scathing about prevailing music fashions, they dared to conquer the United States – not to become part of music's mainstream, but for the mainstream to come to them. Their big anthems and big performances put them at the top of music's pile just five years after their debut album was released.

But, as Bono sings in the song 'The Fly': "ambition bites the nail of success", and at the peak of their powers they executed a creative U-turn to dream it all up again in a run-down studio in Berlin. This constant reinvention and reupholstering of their sound has allowed them to remain relevant to successive generations of music fans.

That they still suffer from performance anxiety and are crippled with nervous trepidation every time a new album or a new tour comes around, speaks of how little they take for granted and how much they still expect from themselves.

More than 150 million albums sold, a record-breaking 22 Grammy Awards and a coruscating career later – both fan and foe have to admit that U2 really are treasures of rock 'n' roll.

BEFORE THEY WERE U2

"Drummer Seeks Musicians to Form Band." This was the note a 14-year-old Laurence Mullen posted on the bulletin board of his school in Dublin on 25 September 1976. Auditions would take place in the kitchen of his parents' house.

Mount Temple School on the north side of Dublin is known for being a progressive and liberal seat of learning. It attracted students who had been thrown out of other schools, which was why Adam Clayton ended up there. It also encouraged self-expression, which suited Paul Hewson (Bono), and it prioritized musical activity, which appealed to David Evans (The Edge). In their teens, Bono and his friends gave each other nicknames. Bono got his from the name of a Dublin hearing-aid shop. He didn't like it at first, but when he found out it was Latin for "good voice" he took to it. He dropped the "Vox" and just became "Bono". The Edge was so christened because he always seemed to be in between one world and another.

Larry Mullen had been playing drums since the age of nine. But drumming alone in his bedroom was beginning to bore him and so in September 1976, he posted his now famous note on the school's bulletin board.

Auditions for the Larry Mullen Band were held in Larry's parents' house in Artane, Dublin – not too far from Mount Temple School. As Larry set up his drum kit, in strolled David Evans and his older brother, Dik. Both could play a bit of guitar, but both were shy and preferred to stay in the background. Adam Clayton – the "bad boy of Mount Temple" – swanned in wearing an eye-catching Afghan coat. Adam could talk the talk and walk the walk and bluffed his way into becoming the band's manager as well as its bass guitarist. Enter Paul Hewson (Bono): a fidgety ball of energy, he was auditioning for the part of guitarist, but it soon became apparent he was an awful

guitar player. Desperately trying to get him away from the guitar, but wanting to keep his presence in the band, Larry and Adam politely suggested he try doing vocals instead.

Mullen was happy with the response to the ad – he was now the leader of a five-piece band. "But the thing is we were only the Larry Mullen Band for about ten minutes," remembers the drummer of that first meeting. "Then Bono walked in and blew any chance I had of being in charge."

Clayton, the most worldly and hippest member of the band, suggested they call themselves "Feedback". When he explained what this musical term meant, the other four members agreed, thinking it sounded good and technical.

Feedback began as a covers band and the first ever song they played together was Peter Frampton's 'Show Me the Way'. Songs by Thin Lizzy and the Eagles were also attempted but with the punk/New Wave scene hitting Dublin, Feedback knew they had to write their own material if they wanted to be taken seriously.

There was an early setback when The Edge's brother, Dik, left to join another band. The now four-piece decided to rename themselves "The Hype" and just 18 months into their fledgling career (and after rehearsing every weekend and after school as many times as they could), they entered into a talent show "to find the most talented and entertaining pop group or showband". It was held in the city of Limerick on 18 March 1978.

Days before the show, they decided on another new band name. Clayton, still the manager, asked a well-known Dublin musician called Steve Averill for help. Adam said he was looking for a name that

sounded a bit like "XTC". Averill came up with ten band name ideas – the last suggestion on the list, "U2", caught Clayton's eye.

U2 won the Limerick talent contest. The first prize was a very generous £500. In addition to the prize money, U2 were given free studio time to record their first demo. Manager Clayton began ringing every Irish music DJ and record company person in Dublin to talk up the talent-show-winning U2. Having been advised that the next step for the band was to secure a recording contract, Clayton decided U2 needed a "real" manager. A Dublin music journalist and early champion of the band, Bill Graham, told Clayton he knew the very man for the job: Paul McGuinness.

McGuinness went to see U2 play two months after the talent show win at a gig in Dublin. Afterwards, he took the band to the pub next door – but the band members were too young to be served alcohol. McGuinness talked to them about the Beatles and the Rolling Stones, about songwriting credits and income distribution. The band members' eyes got wider as McGuinness started talking about what they should do with all the money that would be flowing in once their debut album went to Number 1. The band were keen but still a bit suspicious of this "old man" (McGuinness was all of 27 when they met) and his "posh" accent. But McGuinness had total belief in U2's potential. And unlike Adam, he seemed to know what he was talking about. A deal was struck. A career was born.

> "This [contest] means we can solve our money problems in a big way, particularly with regard to equipment. Now we hope to be able to buy a van." Bono

OPPOSITE, LEFT: Fresh-faced but determined to make a name for themselves, U2 strike a pose at an early gig in 1976.

OPPOSITE, RIGHT: The Dublin boys started out as a covers band by the name of Feedback. Days prior to appearing in a Limerick talent contest, the band changed their name to U2.

TOP: In the early days, sometimes Bono's best friend Guggi stood in for Larry Mullen for band photo shoots.

RIGHT: Bono and The Edge pose for press shots in Dublin's Trinity College.

THE DANDELION GIGS

Just out of school and with no record label deal, U2 spent 1979 playing anywhere that would have them. Bono squeezed himself into a pair of too tight leather trousers, took mime classes, applied some eye-liner and borrowed some stage dance moves from Siouxsie and the Banshees. The venues: car parks, mainly.

There was a plan. To get a record deal, you had to play live. And you had to be better than all the other Dublin bands playing live in order to get the London record company A&R man to open his chequebook. U2 may have been short on songs and experience, but they weren't lacking in confidence. Whenever a member of the all-conquering Boomtown Rats or Thin Lizzy was back in Dublin, a member of U2 would be delegated to hunt him down and get first-hand advice on "how to make it".

While other punk/New Wave bands of the time stuck to the same basic musical template, U2 clearly had ideas above their station. Bono would jump into the audience, climb up on lighting rigs and if needs be, get in a fist fight with the skinhead gangs who always tried to break their gigs up. He was an oddity – a frontman who seemed to think he was performing to 100,000 people when there were only a handful in the audience. His mime lessons were paying off and he would conjure up different characters for different songs – much to the bemusement of Dublin's punk audiences.

The band now had an arsenal of about 12 originally composed songs. A demo tape had been recorded but didn't impress. Manager Paul McGuinness convinced the band that they should do a residency in a particular venue; the idea was that more and more people would come to the gigs until such a buzz had developed around the band, they would simply have to get a record deal.

The Dandelion Market on Dublin's St Stephen's Green, or Dando as it was known, was the venue of choice. A hippy/punk affair that appealed to the youth with its exotic stalls, there was a big shed at the back where bands would play afternoon gigs at the weekend. Peter Frampton, Thin Lizzy and Eagles covers were now part of the past and U2 instead had a punk-influenced sound that was inspired by the Ramones, Joy Division and the Clash.

That summer of 1979 shaped U2 as a live band. Their residency at the Dandelion Market became the talk of the town. Early songs such as 'Stories for Boys' (which they resurrected for their Glastonbury 2011 appearance) and 'Shadows and Tall Trees' had potential, but it was the way the band commanded attention from audiences that marked them out. With Larry, Edge and Adam all statuesque on stage, it was left to Bono to animate the show. He was, as an early U2 single had it, 'Out of Control'. Possessed by rock 'n' roll demons he jumped, ran, screamed and flung himself around the stage with abandon. There were holes in the makeshift stage, sometimes the sound worked, sometimes it didn't, the lighting went on and off at will. But they had a presence. Anything could happen at a U2 show – and frequently did.

> **"There were bands who looked better than us, played better than us and wrote better songs than us. But nothing was ever going to stop me picking up a microphone and trying to say something through U2's music."** Bono

By the end of the summer their plan had worked. CBS Records (now Sony) decided to release a 12-inch EP featuring three of the band's best songs for the Irish market. Such was the buzz for the release by this band from the Dando that a local DJ held a phone-in competition on his rock show so fans could vote for which of the three songs should go on the A side. Live favourite 'Out of Control' became the band's first-ever single release, backed by 'Stories for Boys' and 'Boy-Girl'. The band were thrilled when it made the Irish singles chart at Number 19. A Top 20 hit for their first single!

It was time for U2 to tour the United Kingdom. In advance of the London dates, Bono warned the *Record Mirror* music newspaper that U2 "wanted to take everything and break everything in the UK – I want people in London to see and hear the band. I want to replace the bands in the charts now because I think we're better."

Their first show at London's Hope and Anchor – where they were billed as "The U2s" – attracted a total of nine people. The Edge broke a string halfway through and the band sulked off early. However, the following night at Covent Garden's Rock Garden, they broke double figures. Paul McGuinness opened a bottle of champagne to celebrate. The band were dejected, but people from Island Records already had their eye on this weird new Irish band. Even back then Island saw the UK as the wrong fit for the band; imagine how American audiences would take to them …

OPPOSITE, TOP & BOTTOM: U2 played one of their first-ever gigs outside Dublin in March 1980. Here the band perform at the Garden of Eden pub in Tullamore, County Offaly in the midlands of Ireland.
LEFT: One of the earliest ever U2 promotional shots. This was taken in Dublin in 1978.
BELOW: U2 at the Country Club in Cork, Ireland on 4 February 1980. The city is home to most of their long-serving live touring crew.

BOY
(1980)

Island Records signed U2 to a five-year recording deal in March 1980. Within days, U2 went into a Dublin studio to record their debut album. Drunk on excitement but sick with nerves, they knew you only get one chance to get it right on your first release.

With some 30 original songs to pick from – most of them tried and trusted live favourites – the band were in confident mood as they assembled in Dublin's Windmill Lane in March for the three-month recording session for *Boy*. But within days, disaster struck. Joy Division's producer, Martin Hannett, who was to be their big-name producer, pulled out after the death of Joy Division's singer, Ian Curtis. A new producer, Steve Lillywhite – fresh from his success working with Siouxsie and the Banshees – arrived as a late replacement and immediately bonded with the band. Together, producer and band sculpted a sonic picture that can still be heard in the band's music today.

Kicking off with 'I Will Follow' (still one of the band's favourite ever songs), the 11-track album succeeded in capturing the urgency of their

live shows. Lyrically the songs dealt with Bono's awkward adolescent years and his search for redemption through U2's music. The inclusion of, by now, older U2 songs such as 'Stories for Boys' and 'Out of Control' pleased their original fans, but it was the newer material which impressed most. Bono was developing as a lyricist and the band were beginning to master their instruments.

Island Records were proved right in their initial summation of the band. While *Boy* didn't make it into the UK charts, it did make it to Number 63 in the US charts.

While their New Wave peer group were busy making albums about existential crisis and the search for meaning in a commercial world, U2's *Boy* was all musical primary colours – bright and optimistic – the sound of teenagers taking their first steps in the adult world. As Bono

was to say later about the album: "It's not about losing your virginity, it's about your virginity."

To summarize the content of the songs, the band used a picture of the six-year-old Peter Rowen on the cover (Rowen's older brother, Guggi, was Bono's best friend growing up). The sleeve designer was Adam's friend, Steve Averill, who had given the band their name a few years previously.

Despite not charting in the UK, the album picked up some rave reviews with most writers noting how "unironic and uncynical" the work was. Such is the band's attachment to their debut album that it remains the only U2 album from which every song (as well as every B-side) has been performed live at least once.

In the US the album's cover was deemed to be too controversial – an image of a naked six-year-old boy might send out the wrong message, the record company believed – and a new cover featuring a distorted image of the four band members was used instead.

With College Radio in the United States getting behind the album's single 'I Will Follow', U2 came to the attention of the country's most important music promoter – Frank Barsalona of Premier Talent. This was the man who booked shows for Led Zeppelin and Bruce Springsteen and his public backing of the band led Bono to believe that U2 could break the US quicker than they could break the UK.

Meanwhile, fans and critics were beginning to wonder about all the Christian imagery and themes being used on the songs. All band members with the exception of Adam were, in fact, practising Christians. Bono, Edge and Larry all firmly believed that their Christianity could be reconciled with the rock 'n' roll world they now lived in. But their faith would soon be tested. The relative success of *Boy* and early inroads into the US market would throw up a conflict. Was faith or music more important to three-quarters of U2?

OPPOSITE: By their later standards, the band's early live shows were rudimentary affairs.
TOP LEFT: The Edge and Bono backstage after having given it their all for a show in Cork, Ireland, in 1979.
TOP RIGHT: U2 in double vision – an early photo shoot, just after the band had completed *Boy*.
RIGHT: At an early London show, Bono dispenses with the microphone. His exuberant stage actions were always a cause of concern for the other three band members.

"We had the chance to leave the country when we signed to Island, but we stayed here because the roots of the band are in Dublin. U2 is an Irish expression." Bono

BONO

He applied for the job of guitarist but was pushed into becoming U2's singer. The frontman has been battered and bruised over the years due to his stage antics but is still coming back for more.

Paul David Hewson was born on 10 May 1960. He got the name Bono Vox from a hearing-aid shop of the same name in Dublin city centre. Bono and his teenage friends were in the habit of giving each other nicknames and before he was christened Bono he was known as "Steinvic von Huyseman". He soon dropped the Vox part of his new nickname (which is Latin for "good voice") and now everyone calls him Bono – even his family.

Never a singer growing up, he initially auditioned to be the guitarist in U2. Not being that great on the instrument, he was politely encouraged to put the guitar down and try out as the lead vocalist. Bono was as surprised as anybody that he could actually hold a note.

The death of his mother when he was just 14 traumatized him – and her image features in many a U2 song. He has frequently said that he turned to music to fill the gap her absence left.

His early work as the band's lyricist was abstract and a touch surreal but during the 1980s, when he found social and political themes to play with in the lyrics, he developed a more bombastic style. It wasn't until the *Achtung Baby* album that he started writing about his own personal experiences. But his most personal and confessional work appears on *Songs of Innocence* in which he literally "sings his life story".

As the band's frontman, Bono included mime routines in his early performances. He was always a loose cannon on stage – climbing up rigging, going walkabout in the audience or jumping off great heights. His improvised antics have been a cause of concern to the other members of the band. He has also badly injured himself on a number of occasions due to his stage behaviour.

During concert rehearsals in Munich in 2010, something Bono did to his back led to him needing emergency surgery which required months of rehabilitation. As a result, the band missed their planned Glastonbury Festival appearance and had to reschedule a whole leg of the 360° tour.

His tenor voice has dramatically strengthened and improved in range over the years. His best ever vocal delivery – according to the singer himself – is on 'Moment of Surrender' from the *No Line on the Horizon* album. He was never properly trained as a singer and he dislikes his vocals on the early U2 albums because he thinks he sings far too high on them. When the band began to play stadia in the mid to late 1980s, he was putting such a strain on his voice due to poor technique that he had to take singing lessons to learn the proper way of projecting his vocals.

Bono has recently revealed that the reason he wears sunglasses all the time is because he has glaucoma. His eyes have always been very sensitive to light – if somebody takes his photograph, he reports that he sees the flash for the rest of the day and his eyes swell up.

His on-stage performances have changed radically over the years. During the 1980s he was hectoring and humourless but as U2's music changed so did he and he now has a more playful side to his performances. Although a perfectionist and somewhat of a control freak when it comes to any representation of the band – whether on record or in concert – Bono has a self-mocking side that has grown over the years.

He married Alison Stewart in 1982. The two had been going out together since they were at Mount Temple School at the same time. They have four grown-up children.

His time outside of U2 is spent on his work as an activist. He has a deep interest in the arts – primarily poetry and the visual arts. He cites Seamus Heaney as being his favourite poet.

Away from the band he has written (with The Edge) a Broadway musical called *Spider-Man: Turn Off the Dark*, which was not only the most expensive Broadway production ever but was marred by bad luck and injuries to the cast. The production closed in 2014. Previously he co-wrote the film *The Million Dollar Hotel* in 2000.

At the end of each U2 tour – such is the amount of energy and adrenaline that he puts into each performance – he needs to "decompress" for two weeks before returning to normality. Any precious time off is spent in his home in the south of France.

ABOVE: Bono, aged 19, strikes a serious pose. The photo remains a personal favourite.

OPPOSITE: (CLOCKWISE FROM TOP) Close-up on Bono in Rome, October 2010, the last show in Europe of the record-breaking 360° tour; playing guitar in Chicago, emotional shows that took place shortly after 9/11 as part of the Elevation tour; pictured in Berlin, July 2009.

OCTOBER

(1981)

The album received mixed reviews and limited radio play. Most bands encounter difficult second album syndrome, but _October_ brought U2 to the very brink – for very personal reasons.

At a show in Portland, Oregon in 1985 Bono asked audience members if any of them had any information about his briefcase which went missing (presumed stolen) when the band played in the city in 1981. He repeated his appeal at another Portland show in 2001. Why was this briefcase so important to him?

Well, at the time it was stolen, the briefcase contained most of the singer's lyrics to their second album, _October_. As a result – with the studio already booked – he had to come up with lyrics on the spot for the songs on the album – a process that put him into a panic. (As a postscript, the stolen briefcase was eventually returned to Bono in Portland in 2004. A woman had found it in the attic of the house she was renting. Twenty-three years too late…)

The album, released in October 1981, was an overtly religious affair with songs such as 'Gloria', 'With a Shout (Jerusalem)' and 'Tomorrow' being directly about their Christian faith. Although not without merit, it stalled the momentum that was building after the release of their debut and its poor reception worried their record label.

Critics began wondering if U2 were a "Christian rock band" and early fans were confused by the album's religious themes. As Bono said at the time: "A lot of people found _October_ hard to accept – I used the word 'rejoice' a lot on it."

There were some plus points, though: the single 'Fire' got the band an appearance on _Top of the Pops_ although as Bono noted they were one of the few bands to appear on the programme only for their song to go down the charts the next week.

Musically the band were growing – Adam's bass playing was a feature of 'Gloria' and Larry came into his own as a drummer/percussionist on 'I Threw a Brick Through a Window'.

On the stream-of-consciousness 'Tomorrow', Bono wrote his most moving and personal lyric to date while detailing his mother's tragic early death when he was just 14. It remains the U2 song that still has the most emotional impact on the singer when he hears it.

The album actually went to Number 11 in the UK charts, but this was in part thanks to a scheme their record label had at the time which involved releasing cassette versions of albums that had music on one side only, leaving the other side free to tape something else on.

The 'Gloria' single saw the band make their first foray into the emerging world of music videos – still one of their best videos, its footage was shot close to the Dublin studio in which the album was recorded.

The worst thing to come out of the _October_ album was The Edge announcing that he wanted to leave U2 because the demands of his

Lillywhite (the producer of their first three albums) was asked to come to Dublin to remix the songs which were intended to be singles. Brian Eno and Daniel Lanois felt slighted by this late move.

A typical last-minute crisis of confidence led the band to reconsider the double album and go for a single album full of potential singles instead. To the last, Bono argued for a double album, but the other band members exercised this veto. When the album was re-released in a newly mastered form in 2007, though, a two-disc format hinted at what the double album would have been.

All the songs that weren't used when the decision was made to make it a single album would all show up as B-sides on *The Joshua Tree*'s singles. One of these – 'The Sweetest Thing' – originally a B-side for 'Where the Streets Have No Name', later became an A-side in 1998 to promote the compilation album *The Best of 1980–1990* and hit Number 1 in Canada and Ireland and Number 3 in the UK.

It was Steve Lillywhite's wife – the singer Kirsty MacColl – who was given the task of selecting the album's track listing. Bono and Edge always argued about which songs should go where on a U2 album, so to avoid another confrontation the job was delegated to MacColl.

The photo shoot for the album cover took place in the Joshua Tree National Park in California. When the photographer, Anton Corbijn, told the band about Joshua trees, Bono was enthralled to find out that the trees were named after the Old Testament prophet Joshua and so *The Two Americas* was retitled *The Joshua Tree*.

If the band look grim on the album cover, that's because the photo shoot took place in December, when even a desert can be freezing cold. They had to remove their coats for the photo and were really feeling the chill because Corbijn kept them in position until he found the shot he wanted.

OPPOSITE: Bono stretches out at the De Kuip stadium in Rotterdam in July 1987. Such was the band's appeal at this time that they were regularly playing to audiences of 50,000-plus each night.
ABOVE LEFT: Bono looks on as Edge plays slide guitar on 12 June 1987 – their first time back at Wembley Stadium, London, since their Live Aid appearance.
ABOVE RIGHT: An official promotional photograph from the *Joshua Tree* album sessions.
RIGHT: Bono hitting the high notes during a show in Las Cruces, Mexico, in April 1987.

"We were offered $23 million to allow 'Where the Streets Have No Name' to be used in a car advertisement. The reason we said no was because we rely on that song for when a U2 live show is going askew. We didn't want some sixteen-year-old kids saying to each other, 'Oh great, they're playing the car ad song.' We didn't want to embarrass our fans." Bono

U2 IN AMERICA

Number 1 singles, multi-million album sales, two Grammy Awards and a big, global, stadium tour. *Time* magazine put them on the cover, calling the band "Rock's Hottest Ticket". U2 had become the biggest rock band in the world.

Record shops in the UK and Ireland opened at midnight on 9 March 1987 in order to cope with the demand for *The Joshua Tree*. Whereas U2 had threatened the top of the charts with previous albums, this time they delivered. The album went to Number 1 in the US for nine weeks and became what was then the fastest-selling album in British chart history. As some indication of how strong the eleven-track album was, five singles were released off it.

The much-respected music critic Robert Hilburn, of the *Los Angeles Times*, wrote that "U2 is what the Rolling Stones ceased being years ago – the greatest rock and roll band in the world." No one had expected quite this level of sales and critical acclaim.

The band had little time to savour their success as *The Joshua Tree* tour began in April and carried on until the end of the year. The band were now playing stadia and suddenly had to deal with logistical, financial and psychological pressures that were never there before. The band scrambled to beef up the U2 organization (touring personnel, press officers, etc.) and were finding out that "celebrity" in the music world was a double-edged sword.

On 27 April, the band became only the fourth-ever rock band (after the Beatles, the Band and the Who) to be featured on the cover of *Time* magazine. It was a massive endorsement of their relatively quick ascent to superstar status.

The Joshua Tree was notable for being released on vinyl, cassette and CD formats. The album was many people's first introduction to the new CD format and if ever an album was recorded to sound good on the new format, this was it.

The year-long *Joshua Tree* tour played to over three million people. Eight of the eleven album songs featured regularly and the bigger the audience, the bigger the message Bono had. Frequently raising social and political concerns from his "pulpit" on the stage, this was Bono becoming the activist – whether talking about the evils of apartheid or the moral bankruptcy of the Reagan administration in the US.

Continuing their fascination with learning about the roots of American music and broadening their own education, the band visited Elvis's Graceland as an act of pilgrimage and Sun Studios in Memphis to record new material. Almost everything on the *Joshua Tree* tour was filmed because the band already had ideas of a cinema film based on their American adventure. Such was the speed with which new material was arriving, a prompt follow-up album was also being confidently discussed.

OPPOSITE, FAR LEFT: U2 in America, 1986.

OPPOSITE, LEFT: The video for 'I Still Haven't Found What I'm Looking For' was filmed in Las Vegas in 1987. The Edge waits for the camera to roll.

TOP: The 360° tour at Giants Stadium, New Jersey in 2009. The tour is the most successful in history.

ABOVE LEFT: The band in Anaheim, California, 2011, for one of the last shows of the 360° tour.

U2's most wildly successful year ever was topped off by winning two Grammy Awards – one for Best Album and another for Best Rock Performance.

But just as the band had previously snatched victory from defeat, now at the very peak of their career old doubts were re-emerging. For the band the live show was always the priority. They always fretted that the bigger their audiences were becoming, how important it was for every single person to make that vital connection with the music. The band had broken through on word of mouth from their lives shows – and they intended to keep their standards just as high, no matter how many people were in the audience.

Larry Mullen summed up the band's doubts succinctly: "We were the biggest, but we weren't the best." It also had been only a few years since three of the band (Bono, The Edge and Larry) had almost walked away from rock 'n' roll because of the conflict it presented with their Christian lifestyle. That had all been resolved – with rock 'n' roll winning out – before the *War* album, but the band were beginning to allude to the fact that the stresses of an enormous stadium tour and their new-found status as rock's hottest ticket led them to embrace the rock musician's lifestyle.

Their lives were now being planned out for them, and they found themselves making commitments to projects they hadn't the time to really think through. The record label was ecstatic with the sales of the album, the fans loved the big, new stadium shows, but the band themselves were wondering just how this New Wave band from Dublin who were all about punk energy and self-expression had strayed from their core principles. They were just about to find out.

ADAM CLAYTON

> " I do realize how unusual it is to be able to play large, sold-out shows 30-plus years into a rock 'n' roll career. I don't take it for granted." Adam Clayton

Adam Clayton was always the bold boy of U2. Expelled from school as a teenager, he talked his way into the band and revelled the most in their success. But now he's the elder statesman of the group.

Born on 13 March 1960, Adam Charles Clayton spent his first five years in Oxfordshire before his family moved to Dublin. By a strange coincidence one of Adam's first friends as a child in Dublin was The Edge (both sets of parents were friends because both had relocated to Dublin from England).

It was always clear that the young Adam was somewhat of a misfit. Aged eight, he was packed off to boarding school, which he disliked intensely because he wasn't the slightest bit interested in sports and the students were not allowed to listen to music on school grounds. After he moved school but was then asked to leave because of his lack of interest, his parents decided to send him to the more liberal, arts-friendly Mount Temple School where Bono, The Edge and Larry were already students.

Just before joining the new school his parents had bought him a bass guitar; Adam didn't know how to play it but liked it because it had a big, fat sound – and it looked cool. At Mount Temple he stood out – he wasn't the best academically and instead would swan around in a big Afghan coat, wearing sunglasses even in the Irish winter, as if he were the rock star he would later become.

He had briefly been in a band before reading Larry Mullen's notice in Mount Temple looking for musicians to form a band. He made a big impression at the audition in Larry's kitchen – he talked about "chords" and "frets" and about "amplifiers" and "feedback". He was immediately in the band for the simple reason that the others thought he knew what he was talking about.

Adam appointed himself manager of the new band. He was impressive – writing to DJs and music journalists and always quick to ask advice from anyone he came across who was even remotely connected with the music industry. When the band began to get serious, though, he ceded this role to Paul McGuinness.

It was difficult for Adam in the early days of U2. He retained a posh, English accent from his time in Oxfordshire and some people took him for being pretentious. Within the band, Bono, The Edge and Larry would frequently hold prayer meetings while on tour – Adam, though, never displayed any interest in the Christian grouping in which they were involved.

His bass playing improved dramatically over the first few years. From '11 o'Clock Tick Tock' to 'New Year's Day', he was developing a melodic style that would go on to underpin the band's later work. He gelled instantly with Larry Mullen as the rhythm section and if his bass playing sometimes goes unheralded it's mainly because it's difficult to be in a band with a virtuoso such as The Edge.

The early U2 were notoriously clean-living, but Adam always did his bit for the rock 'n' roll cause. Quite the party animal, he was arrested in 1989 for possession of marijuana. He avoided conviction by making a sizeable donation to charity.

But his drinking was beginning to get out of hand, particularly on the Zoo TV tour. He was so drastically hungover in Sydney in 1993 that he was unable to play that night's show. And it was an important show: the next night the band were filming their Zoo TV live DVD. This was the first time any member of U2 had missed a show and such was the shock and disappointment felt by Clayton that he immediately sought treatment for his alcohol problem. He has been sober ever since.

Known for his gentlemanly ways and his polite, good manners, he's had his fair share of blows. In 2012 his long-time housekeeper was sentenced to seven years' imprisonment after it was reported she had misappropriated 2.8 million euros of Clayton's money.

He has had a series of relationships over the years – including an engagement to the model Naomi Campbell. He has a child from a relationship that is now over and in 2013 he married the Brazilian model Mariana Teixeira de Carvalho.

Somewhat of the wise old man of U2 these days, Adam Clayton has travelled the furthest of all the members of the band. Now quietened down considerably since his rock 'n' roll excess days, he has found perspective and wisdom and has become an even more valued member of the band than he was previously.

Above: Adam during the Joshua Tree tour; his English accent won him the nickname "The Posh One".
Opposite: (clockwise from top left) an early shot of Adam, when he was also manager; taking a break during rehearsals for the Joshua Tree tour; Adam in Dublin, in the days of New Wave; in Toronto, for the 360° tour.

> ### "Can you imagine your second album, the difficult second album, and it's all about God?" Bono

faith and the rock 'n' roll lifestyle could not be reconciled. The Edge, Bono and Larry were all members of a Christian group known as the Shalom Fellowship and pressure had been put on band members to renounce their rock 'n' roll lives.

When The Edge informed manager Paul McGuinness of his decision to leave, there was pandemonium because the tour dates to support the album had already been booked. Displaying a dry sense of humour that stood him in good stead as U2's long-term manager, McGuinness said to The Edge: "If God had something he wanted to say about this tour, he should have raised his hand a little earlier."

In time, Bono, Larry and The Edge left Shalom and devoted themselves to U2. It was a very close call, though, particularly for The Edge. But just as personal matters got resolved, there was another threat to the band looming on the horizon. Island Records were not happy with the poor sales figures of *October*. U2 would have to record a hit third album or the deal was off. The pressure was on.

OPPOSITE, FAR LEFT: The band in concert in 1981 shortly after the release of their underperforming second album, *October*.

OPPOSITE, LEFT: The October tour hit San Francisco in November 1981. For three of the band, the tour was a struggle to reconcile their Christian beliefs with a rock 'n' roll lifestyle.

ABOVE: Bono and The Edge at the Torhout Festival in Belgium, 1982. From a musical Welsh family, The Edge is a fine singer in his own right.

RIGHT: In June 1981, U2 played at one of their first festivals: the PinkPop Festival in the Netherlands.

THE MAKING OF *WAR*

(1983)

When U2's third album was released, it knocked Michael Jackson's *Thriller* off the top of the UK charts. This was the big time. Just how big could this band get?

When U2 reconvened to record *War* in 1982, the band were under pressure. Their second album hadn't performed as well as expected, the early career plan to storm the US market had been torn up and the tensions between their religious faith and their commitment to the band's cause had only just been resolved.

But there was fire in the quartet's bellies when they began *War*. They knew they were up against the wall, some fans had been let down by *October* and the record company were getting anxious for a more commercial sounding record.

War began with Bono penning a love song to his long-time girlfriend, Alison Stewart (the two had been going out together since meeting at Mount Temple School). Married shortly after the *War* sessions began, Bono wrote 'New Year's Day' about his new bride – "I want to be with you, be with you, night and day." However, the song slowly changed and in the studio it became reshaped into an anthem of sorts for the Polish Solidarity Movement – who, at the time, were standing up to Russian-imposed Communist rule in their country.

'New Year's Day' was to prove significant for the band: as a single from the album, it became the band's first hit outside of Ireland and the UK and introduced the band, through massive radio play, to European audiences. It remains the fifth most played song ever on all the U2 tours.

While *Boy* was about adolescent dreams and *October* about spiritual questioning, *War* was in many ways U2's political album. 'Sunday Bloody Sunday' addressed the violence and political turmoil in Northern Ireland while other songs drew upon disturbing events in then apartheid South Africa and the continuing war in the Middle East.

As a complete piece of work, *War* sounded rougher and more urgent than anything they had recorded before. This was mainly due to The Edge using far fewer guitar effects (on previous albums he had drowned his guitar sound with delay and echo) and going for a more aggressive sound. Larry Mullen's military-style drumming added to the directness of the sound.

The cover of the album reflected the band's new musical approach. Peter Rowen, the six-year-old boy from the cover of the *Boy* album, returned as a stern-looking nine-year-old for *War*. As Bono explained: "Instead of putting guns and tanks on the cover, we've put a child's face. War can also be a mental thing, an emotional thing between lovers. It doesn't have to be a physical thing."

It was in fact a personal "war" between The Edge and his then girlfriend, Aislinn O'Sullivan (later his wife) that led to the album's stand-out moment. Following a row with Aislinn and still worried about the band's seemingly faltering career, Edge channelled all his frustrations into the guitar riff that held up 'Sunday Bloody Sunday'.

There were still songs influenced by their religious faith. Both 'Drowning Man' and '40' have lyrics taken directly from the Bible.

> **"Everywhere you looked, from the Falklands to the Middle East and South Africa, there was war. By calling the album *War*, we were giving people a slap in the face and at the same time getting away from the cosy image a lot of people had of U2."** Bono

War also began the now sacred U2 album ritual of not finishing an album until literally the very last second. The final song to be recorded for the album was '40'. The song takes its title from the fact that it was written in ten minutes, then recorded in ten minutes, then mixed in ten minutes and then played back for ten minutes in the studio just as U2's recording time for *War* was up. For a song written so quickly, '40' became an important live moment for the band. It was used for years as the closing song at U2 concerts with the band walking off one by one until just the audience were left to continue singing the song's refrain – "How long to sing this song?"

OPPOSITE: Bono on stage during the second date of the War tour in Manchester, 1982. Such was the album's success that they were playing in clubs at the start but finished, two years later, playing in arenas.

ABOVE: U2 performing on Channel 4's music programme *The Tube* in 1983.

RIGHT: Bono gets the audience to sing along during a show early in the War tour.

FAR RIGHT: *War* – both the album and the tour – transformed U2's fortunes, taking them from New Wave misfits to serious contenders. At the tour's end, Bono looks more than happy.

WAR
(1983)

War did not just top the charts but refined the band musically and lyrically. All the pointers for the band's later career are to be found in this still very fondly remembered work.

Nerves were settled when the first single from *War*, 'New Year's Day', became a Top 10 single in the UK one month ahead of the album's release. A further boost came when the prestigious *Rolling Stone* magazine singled out 'Sunday Bloody Sunday' as evidence that "U2 were capable of deep and meaningful song writing".

Still one of their signature songs, 'Sunday Bloody Sunday' was not without controversy. The Bloody Sunday the song speaks about refers to British troops shooting and killing unarmed civil rights protesters in Derry, Northern Ireland in 1972. The band had concerns that they were seen to be taking sides in Northern Ireland's bitter sectarian conflict and Bono took to introducing the song when they played it live with the words: "This is not a rebel song." Bono waving a white flag during the song's performance on stage became an early emblem of the band.

Musically, the album was an education for the band. Producer Steve Lillywhite tried to get Larry Mullen to use a click track (audio cues through headphones to synchronize the beat) during its recording,

but Mullen resisted until a chance meeting with a fellow musician persuaded him otherwise. Mullen still uses a click track today.

War was the first U2 album to feature additional musicians, with Steve Wickham (of the Waterboys) providing electric violin and backing vocals provided by Kid Creole's singers, the Coconuts.

The band were on an extensive UK tour when news filtered in that the album had gone to Number 1 in the charts. Because they were signed to a UK label, this was doubly significant – it was proof that they could produce hit albums, but it also showed the label that they could actually stay living and recording in Dublin (much against the label's wishes) while still conquering the UK charts.

War's most lasting and much overlooked significance was that it demonstrated to the band just how potent any form of political message (however oblique) could be in rock music. Bono, for one, was interested in exploring further socio-political commentary through the band's music even if the other three members were more reluctant.

OPPOSITE: At the San Bernardino festival in 1983, U2 appeared to an audience of 125,000 people – at that point, their biggest yet. The festival was transmitted live from California on MTV.

LEFT: During their set, Bono distinguished himself by singing 'The Electric Co.' while scaling the stage's proscenium arch – all 30 metres (100 feet) of it.

BELOW LEFT: U2 in full technicolor glory during a break from the War tour.

BELOW RIGHT: Adam Clayton stands guard over Bono during the San Bernardino festival.

The seeds of the singer's future role as an activist on the global stage were sown during the recording of the *War* album.

With MTV now becoming a powerful force in the music world, the band upped their game with the release of the video for 'New Year's Day'. Shot in Sweden in December, the weather was so cold that the singer could barely keep his mouth open. But the resultant work got them on to MTV and convinced the band that the visual image was becoming just as important as the audio message. This realization was to reach its full creative fruition with the later Zoo TV tour.

For all these reasons, *War* remains one of the most important albums of U2's career. They still play these songs live on each and every tour, and if you talk to the band now they will reminisce fondly about how this era in their professional lives was perhaps their best ever. They were going to Number 1, selling out tours and receiving acclaim in musical territories that had hitherto proved resistant to their music.

Bono now had anthems to sing on stage; songs which were already radio hits. The album had been vital for The Edge, Adam and Larry in terms of moving them on from their early, rudimentary smash-and-grab New Wave style. All the pieces were beginning to fit together.

For the *War* tour, the band sought out the services of the stage and lighting designer Willie Williams. Now recognized as one of the leading artists in his field, Williams has been responsible for every U2 tour since and his contribution cannot be ignored.

With three albums under their belt, the band had a setlist that was good enough to get them up to playing arenas. Bono was increasingly feeling that these new songs were "message" songs and he was desperate to stay on the road for as long as possible – not just to keep Island Records happy by increasing sales of the album but also for U2 to become a formidable live act. And Bono, as the band well knew, is at his most dangerous when he believes he has something to say.

With the band firing on all cylinders, the *War* tour crossed the Atlantic to America and everything was about to change – again.

"Music can be more than pop, its possibilities are great. Music has changed me. It can change a generation." Bono

TOUR LEGENDS: UNDER A BLOOD RED SKY

"U2 Declare War" read the tour poster. Over the course of the near worldwide War tour, the band moved up from clubs to halls to arenas. Along the way, there was a memorable show at the Red Rocks Amphitheater in Colorado.

The *War* tour began in Dundee on 26 February 1983 and ended in Tokyo on 30 November 1983. That sentence alone tells you all you need to know about the ground they travelled in less than a year. A series of pre-*War* tour dates in December 1982 – two months before the album came out – saw them getting to grips with the new songs live. The UK tour from February through to early April with shows almost every night left them tight and taut as a live band before the tour moved to the United States.

As they hit the big urban centres of Boston, New York and Chicago (all cities with sizeable Irish populations) in May 1983, they were playing out of their skins and receiving the best reviews of their career. The *New York Times* immediately singled out Bono as "a riveting public personality, leaping and crawling all over the stage and above it into the scaffolding" (which was almost word for word how Irish music journalists had reviewed his performance at the early Dandelion Market shows four years previously).

The success of the gigs meant that the *War* album stayed in and around the Top 20 album charts in the US for the duration of the tour. On 5 June the band played at the Red Rocks Amphitheater – a natural amphitheatre in the Rocky Mountains and a favourite of many a band.

The show shouldn't have taken place – there was torrential rain on the day and flash flood warnings were issued. But a lot of money had been invested in culling a live album and live video film from the show and fans had walked through pouring rain to get to the venue, so the band persevered. It was so cold that evening that Edge could barely play his guitar and thankfully the large banks of mist concealed all the empty seats – many fans had just assumed the show had been called off because of the rain storms. Only half of the 9,000-odd seats were taken on the night.

The subsequent live album was called *Under a Blood Red Sky* (a line taken from 'New Year's Day'). The album cover – and film – is covered in crimson mist as a result of the rain and the lights illuminating the amphitheatre. Larry Mullen has always believed that the weather actually made the show.

Featuring old songs such as '11 O'Clock Tick Tock' and the singles from *War*, the album captured both the live passion and the sky-scraping ambition of a band on the way up.

The live version of 'Sunday Bloody Sunday' has been cited as one of *Rolling Stone* magazine's "50 Moments That Changed the History of Rock and Roll", such was its dazzling impact on the night. The Red Rocks show is still regularly voted one of the gigs of the 1980s.

Before the show and live album release (which was out a few months later) U2 were still a marginal, College Radio band in the US. But Red Rocks brought them to the attention of not just the MTV generation (the music channel regularly featured the full live video show) but also convinced many that the band were now ready to make the leap to arenas and stadia.

During the 1997 PopMart tour the band did consider returning to Red Rocks for a second show but were talked out of it as being a no-win situation – the thinking being they could never re-capture that particular moment or the same rain storm.

In the summer months of 1983, U2 played their first big European festival dates and their biggest ever Dublin show at the Phoenix Park Racecourse in the city. They ended the eventful *War* tour with their first-ever shows in Hawaii and Japan.

The only worrying aspect of the *War* tour was the ever-present fear that Bono would harm himself while climbing up to the ceiling at almost every show. The Edge later confessed that Bono "scared the shit out of me" by climbing lighting rigs to display his white flag. But as the band already knew: it was too late to stop him now.

> **"We're not just another English fashion band passing through. We're an Irish band and we're here to stay."** Bono

ABOVE: Between April and June 1983, the War tour broke U2 into the US mainstream.
OPPOSITE: (CLOCKWISE FROM TOP LEFT) The Edge with a favourite guitar; Bono now says he was "too preachy" at this time; Larry Mullen learned to how to be a rock 'n' roll percussionist thanks to *War* – both album and tour; Adam Clayton c. 1983, when he was a party animal.

THE EDGE

A remarkable guitarist who has had his own style since Day One, The Edge is the creative driving force behind the group's music. And the least likely U2 member to start an argument.

David Howell Evans was born in London to Welsh parents on 8 August 1961. When he was a year old the family relocated to Dublin due to his father, an engineer, receiving a promotion. He was given the nickname "The Edge" by friends of Bono when he was a teenager. Depending on who you talk to, he got his nickname either from his sharp, edge-like facial features or because his shyness meant he used to stay in the background – on the edge of what was happening around him.

He and his older brother Richard (Dik) were both interested in the guitar. They had bought a second-hand acoustic guitar at a jumble sale for £1 while in their early teens and learnt basic chord structures from plonking away on it.

When Larry Mullen's now famous notice went up on the board at Mount Temple School, both Edge and Dik went to the first audition and both were accepted into the band. Dik Evans played only a few shows with the band (when they were still known as the Hype), but there was always a feeling that the musical unit would work better as a four-piece so Dik was "phased out" – as the band put it. The Edge still remembers the heartbreak of telling his brother the news.

Even on the band's first album, *Boy*, it was immediately clear that this was no ordinary guitar player. The Edge's playing style was the very opposite to what a lead guitarist usually plays. He favoured a minimalist style, which allowed him to explore different textures. He never played that many notes but did use delay effects which created a more ambient sound. So out of synch with then prevailing guitar playing styles was his approach that you could immediately recognize a U2 song just from his guitar parts.

While his playing style is minimal, his use of effects and pedals really fills out his sound. His short and sharp approach was very much of the New Wave era of music influenced by bands such as the Skids. He cites guitarists Tom Verlaine (from the band Television) and Irish blues guitarist Rory Gallagher as his main inspirations. He also has impressive keyboard skills.

A fine singer in his own right, he is the band's backing vocalist – frequently harmonizing to Bono's voice. He sings lead vocals on 'Van Diemen's Land' from *Rattle and Hum* and 'Numb' from *Zooropa*. On later U2 tours he sang lead vocals on 'Sunday Bloody Sunday'.

He released his own solo album in 1986 – a soundtrack album for a film called *Captive*. On the song 'Heroine' from the album, the vocals are supplied by a young Sinead O'Connor.

Now regarded as one of the best popular music guitarists in the world, he played arguably his best work on the *Achtung Baby* album – particularly on 'The Fly' and 'Mysterious Ways'.

He married his school girlfriend Aislinn O'Sullivan in 1983. The couple had three children before separating in 1990. He met the choreographer Morleigh Steinberg when she appeared as a belly dancer on the Zoo TV tour. They have two children and were married in 2002.

He appeared in the music documentary film *It Might Get Loud* (2009), which explored his guitar life as well as those of Jimmy Page and Jack White.

Following the 2005 Hurricane Katrina cyclone, he helped set up Music Rising – a charity that helped to provide replacement musical instruments for musicians in the New Orleans area who had lost everything. Following one of his daughters successfully battling against cancer, he became very involved with the Angiogenesis Foundation – a research organization that looks at new scientific techniques to treat cancer and other serious illnesses. He is one of the directors of the foundation.

While hiking with his wife in the Malibu area of California shortly after they were married, the couple fell in love with a particular area of land which they bought. For the last eight years The Edge has been in talks with the Coastal Commission of California about his plans to build five houses on the land.

Known for his placid manner, all three of his bandmates cite him as the real key to the band's success.

ABOVE: Exclusive! The Edge without his hat – an early shot of the virtuoso guitarist.

OPPOSITE: (CLOCKWISE FROM TOP) Slane Castle was the backdrop for a homecoming gig in September 2001; during the October tour, he struggled with his religious beliefs; Toronto for 2009's 360° tour; in Toronto again, one of the band's favourite cities, for the Joshua Tree tour; .

THE UNFORGETTABLE FIRE (1984)

Living together in a castle in the middle of Ireland, the band decided to abruptly change gears: no more rock music, time for a soft, ambient, arty album. Eyebrows were raised.

There was never going to be a *War* Part 2. U2 felt they were being put into a "sloganeering rock band" box and so, in their biggest creative swerve to date, they dispensed with Steve Lillywhite – the producer of their first three albums – and got Brian Eno and Daniel Lanois in to work on *The Unforgettable Fire*.

It had now become abundantly clear that U2 were a stubborn if not refractory group. They could have scaled the heights of stadium rock music by continuing in the same vein as *War*. But they wanted to explore texture and sounds that were new to them. For the first time they had the financial clout (due to the success of *War* and *Under a Blood Red Sky*) to dictate terms to their record company.

Living together in Slane Castle in the middle of Ireland (which was later to become the scene of some of their biggest-ever shows), they wanted to confuse and confound with a more avant-garde-sounding work, an album of impressionistic flourishes as opposed to the harsh and direct guitar rock of the album that preceded it.

In the castle's gothic ballroom they started and stopped songs, tried different sounds and effects and began from scratch more than once. Brian Eno just kept the tapes recording all the time.

Their label boss, Chris Blackwell, publicly fretted that Eno "would bury them under a layer of avant-garde nonsense" but that was a risk that U2 were not only willing to take but actually relished.

Worries that they would disappear into a fog of self-indulgent experimentation were allayed by the first two tracks on the album. 'A Sort of Homecoming' and 'Pride (In the Name of Love)' were sonically more expansive than anything they had tried before but still contained melodic strength and commercial appeal. Elsewhere the album contained loosely arranged instrumentals and poetic-sounding sketches.

"Certainly not an album of hit singles" chorused almost every review of the time, but as a complete work *The Unforgettable Fire* impressed on many levels – the band were growing musically, taking chances and were ploughing a new musical furrow. It did help matters that the album contained their biggest-ever hit single in 'Pride' – a Top 5 hit in the UK. The song was written as a tribute for civil rights leader Martin Luther King Jr and remains one of the band's best-known tracks.

It also soon became abundantly clear that certain album songs, most notably 'Bad' (a song about heroin addiction in the area of Dublin Bono was from), took on a whole new life when played live. The full visceral effect of 'Bad' is only to be felt when Bono is improvising over and around it in a live setting. On the album, 'Bad' is six minutes long; when played live it rarely comes in under the twelve-minute mark.

Perhaps the most important aspect of the album is that it was the bridge album that got them from *War* to *The Joshua Tree*. And the band were to pull off this type of musical reinvention later on when they followed up *Rattle and Hum* with *Achtung Baby*.

Typical U2, then – a deliberately uncommercial album that gave them their biggest-ever commercial hit single. They kept the music critics on side; they pacified their record label and only enhanced their reputation with an album that people (including the band themselves) had real concerns about.

And in time-honoured U2 tradition, 12 days before the album was due to go to the pressing plant, only 60 per cent of *The Unforgettable Fire* was finished. The band worked 20-hour days to finish it off. The mad scramble actually paid off – a lot of the songs here sound like incomplete sketches, which was the very effect they wanted in the first place.

Less than a year after the album's release, U2 had the chance to showcase their new songs in front of the biggest music television audience of all time when the Live Aid charity concert was staged at Wembley Stadium in July 1985. What could go wrong?

OPPOSITE: A photograph from 1985, which eerily resembles how they would be shot for *The Joshua Tree* two years later.

ABOVE LEFT: In the hills outside Dublin during a break in the recording of *The Unforgettable Fire* in 1984.

ABOVE RIGHT: The Edge on stage in Sydney, Australia in September 1984 during the Unforgettable Fire tour. Songs that sounded "unfinished" on the album came into their own when played live.

RIGHT: In Rotterdam on 30 October 1984 as the Unforgettable Fire tour hits Europe.

"With Steve Lillywhite, we were strict with the songs; if they veered off course we would pull them back. With Brian Eno and Daniel Lanois, we were more interested in watching where a song went and then chasing it." Adam Clayton

LIVE AID AND U2

Simple really: two billion people are watching the Live Aid show, U2 are to play three songs including their new single 'Pride'. This is their most important show ever.

When Bob Geldof was organizing the giant Live Aid music concert at Wembley Stadium in July 1985, he was determined to have U2 on the bill – even if their then status didn't actually warrant an appearance. As a fellow Dubliner, Geldof loved U2 and Bono had flown across the Atlantic at a minute's notice to help out with vocals on the 'Do They Know It's Christmas' single from the previous December, which Geldof and Midge Ure had written to raise funds for Ethiopian famine relief.

U2 are control freaks when it comes to their live appearances. They don't like ceding control to anyone other than their immediate tried and trusted light and sound personnel. When informed there would be no time for a soundcheck, the band panicked but resolved to perform their three-song set to the best of their ability.

Opening song 'Sunday Bloody Sunday' worked well – clearly Bono was feeding off the energy of the 75,000-plus Wembley audience. "We're a band from Dublin. Like all cities it has its good and it has its bad – this is a song called 'Bad'," says Bono, introducing their second song. Six minutes in, when the band should be getting ready to start thinking about going into 'Pride', Bono has a rush of blood to the head.

Leaping down off the stage, he gestures to a girl in the audience to climb over the security barrier and join him on stage. Trying to help her, he jumps further down so he's on ground level – way out of sight of the band on stage – and continues trying to extract various audience members from beyond the security barrier.

On stage, The Edge, Adam and Larry don't know what is going on. Worried glances are exchanged as they keep on playing the song. Had Bono decided to cut the set short and was now back in the dressing room? What were the band to do in front of their biggest-ever television audience?

Larry Mullen remembers the experience as "excruciating", saying "We didn't know whether we should stop, we didn't know where he was; we didn't know if he had fallen." The band were well used to Bono climbing up scaffolding and going into the audience from as far back as their Dandelion Market days, but this was different – he was out of their visual range and nothing was coming through on his microphone.

Eventually Bono reappeared. There was still a few minutes left to play 'Pride' but instead the singer chose to continue with 'Bad', adding in improvised lyrical excerpts from the Rolling Stones' 'Ruby Tuesday' and Lou Reed's 'Satellite of Love'. When Bono realized their allotted

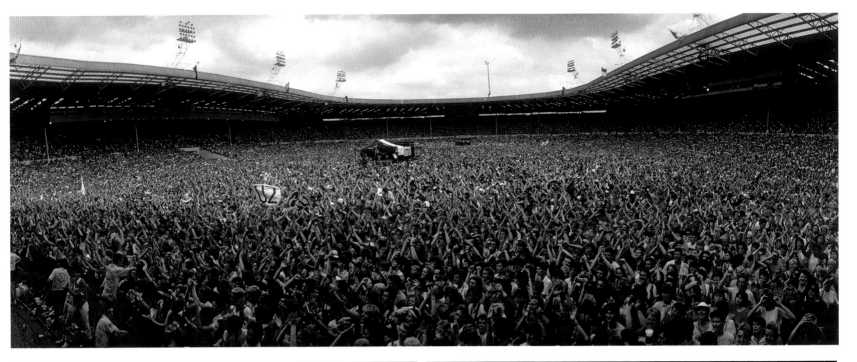

time is up, he left the stage without making eye contact with any of the band.

In the dressing room afterwards, there is a furious row. Bono's antics had meant they hadn't played 'Pride', an important song to them at the time and his self-indulgence had ruined U2's big global moment. Bono was to claim later that the band were so incandescent with rage they wanted to sack him.

Back in Ireland, a distraught Bono got into his car and drove deep into the Irish countryside, feeling he had let everyone down – U2 most of all. He made sure he was out of touch because he didn't want to face another band interrogation about why he had ruined the performance.

But as the days went by, it transpired that everyone was talking about the band's performance in a positive and enthusiastic way. By straying off script, Bono (still not that well-known at this stage) had become a hot topic. Outside Queen's performance later that evening, U2's set became *the* Live Aid moment – the one people still remember best.

Not for the first time, U2 had forged triumph out of apparent failure. That afternoon at Wembley Stadium was the moment U2 became a truly global band.

OPPOSITE: (CLOCKWISE FROM TOP) Bono on stage at Live Aid; fellow Dubliner Bob Geldof (left) fought to get U2 on to the Wembley bill; as Live Aid comes to a close, Bono joins George Michael, Freddie Mercury and others to sing 'Do They Know It's Christmas?'.
ABOVE: Rockin' all over the world – almost 75,000 people enjoyed U2's performance, Bono's dramatic walkabout included.
LEFT: Bono is on stage to survey the scene while performing 'Bad'.

THE MAKING OF THE JOSHUA TREE (1987)

With each of the four previous U2 albums very different to the one before, expectations were running high for their fifth release. But those expectations didn't allow for the fact that the band were about to record one of the best-selling rock albums of all time.

The Joshua Tree began in Ethiopia. A few weeks after Live Aid, Bono and Ali travelled to the African country for six weeks to see for themselves the impact of the devastating famine. Unable to sleep one night, Bono sat up in his tent, reached for an airsickness bag (the only thing he could find to write on) and wrote: "I want to run, I want to hide, I want to tear down the walls that hold me inside." When The Edge later came up with the music to accompany these lyrics they had the album's centre point – 'Where the Streets Have No Name'.

With Brian Eno and Daniel Lanois invited back to produce the album, the band reassembled in a big Georgian house on the outskirts of Dublin in January 1986 to start work. It was called Danesmoate House, and Adam Clayton took such a shine to the place that he bought it later on – and still lives there today. It was the "non-studio" atmosphere of the house which led to some very relaxed sessions. Co-producer Daniel Lanois felt he was getting a particular sound from the rooms in the house and everyone – for once on a U2 album – seemed happy.

They knew they wanted tighter songs than were on *The Unforgettable Fire*. If many of those songs were deliberately left open-ended, here the focus was on conventional structures. The recording sessions were marked by the band emphasizing the primary colours of rock music – guitar, bass and drums.

Bono wanted the album to be about the United States – a country that they had spent more time in than in Ireland over the previous few years due to incessant coast-to-coast touring. The album was to be called *The Two Americas* and would deal with "hot button" themes from the foreign news headlines of the day. It was determined early on that this would be the band's first double album. Given the broadness of the subject matter there were enough songs there and the band felt on this, their fifth LP, the timing was right for a double album.

Two key events helped shape the songwriting. The band broke off recording to take part in the Amnesty International Conspiracy of Hope tour in the summer of 1986 in the US, which gave them political material that would find its way into the songs. And just as Bono and Ali had travelled to Ethiopia previously to see what was going on with their own eyes, this time the couple travelled to Nicaragua and El Salvador to witness the effects of US military intervention in these countries.

It was a love/hate album. The band had a deep appreciation of all aspects of US culture and admired the country's dramatic geographical spaces but were appalled by the Ronald Reagan years and particularly by US military intervention in Central America. The latter sentiment informed the songs 'Bullet the Blue Sky' and 'Mothers of the Disappeared'. But in there too was an acknowledgement of

what the country was to many generations of Irish emigrants and how it was the US and not the UK who really put the band on a pedestal. 'With or Without You' was Bono's love letter to his wife, Ali. Despite being newlyweds, the couple didn't see that much of each other due to the band's touring demands and Bono articulated his frustration through the song.

The album has rootsy/blues touches for the very reason that the band had realized that their musical education began and ended with the New Wave music scene that first fired them up as teenagers in Dublin. With U2 now under so much of a media spotlight, they were frightened by how little they knew about popular music's history, and songs such as 'I Still Haven't Found What I'm Looking For' even found the band incorporating elements of Gospel music into their sound. The song is notable for Bono expressing his doubts about religion.

'I Still Haven't Found …' is Larry Mullen's song. He came up with a very original beat which allowed the band to go walkabout musically and the result was the most non-U2-sounding song to date. Bono sings at the very top of his range over the beat and by nailing something so different early on the song anchored the album and gave the band the confidence to explore a more rootsy style.

Above: Bono and The Edge pour it all into 'Bullet the Blue Sky' from the acclaimed album *The Joshua Tree*.

Opposite: The Joshua Tree tour made U2 "rock's hottest ticket" according to a cover story that appeared in *Time* magazine in 1987.

"The idea we had for the album was simply: let's actually write songs. We wanted the record to be less vague, atmospheric and impressionistic than *The Unforgettable Fire* – to make it more straightforward, focused and concise."

The Edge on *The Joshua Tree*

THE JOSHUA TREE

(1987)

A double album to be called *The Two Americas*. There were plenty of twists and turns – and The Edge dancing around in triumph – before the album now known as *The Joshua Tree* was finished.

On the song 'Running to Stand Still', Bono returned to the lyrical theme of 'Bad' with another exploration of the ruinous effects of heroin in Dublin – some people Bono knew in the area he grew up in had succumbed to the numbing qualities of the drug.

The music for 'Where the Streets Have No Name' came about when The Edge – in his Dublin home – wanted to "conjure up the ultimate U2 live song" for the album. Playing around with keyboards, guitars and a drum machine, he came up with what he still believes is "the most amazing guitar part" of his life. To celebrate his breakthrough, he danced around his house in joy, punching the air in triumph. By the time Bono finished the lyrics he had started in Ethiopia to 'Where the Streets Have No Name', the song had changed to the extent that it was now about Belfast – a city where the name of the street on which you

lived signalled what part of the sectarian divide you belonged to. Bono was the son of a Protestant mother and a Catholic father and could never get his head around religious sectarianism.

On the song 'Red Hill Mining Town', Bono engaged with the bitter and divisive coal miners' strike in Britain. It was partly inspired by meeting and interviewing Bob Dylan and learning more about the folk/protest music scene. It's one of U2's most curious songs: the band felt it was one of the strongest tracks on the album and had planned to release it as the second single, but when push came to shove they reappraised it as being "over-produced and unfinished". It remains the only song from the album that the band have never played live.

The only slight note of discord in what was one of the band's most relaxed and happiest album recording sessions was when Steve

RATTLE AND HUM

(1988)

Still dizzy from the success of *The Joshua Tree*, U2 stayed in American musical mode for their next album and also saw their first film hit cinemas. How big could this get for them?

The joint live album/film version had worked so well for the band with *Under a Blood Red Sky* that they decided to repeat the process five years later with *Rattle and Hum*. At this stage the band's whole existence involved touring *The Joshua Tree* around the US and selling more and more records and filling out bigger and bigger stadia on a weekly basis.

Film director Phil Joanou pitched the idea of a feature-length film of the band, which would focus on their live shows. It helped that a recent recording session in Memphis had yielded some strong new material, and the band were keen to release a mainly live album that had the added attraction of original new studio material.

For the bulk of the concert footage in the film, the band returned as close as possible to the Red Rocks Amphitheater in Colorado by using footage from two indoor shows in nearby Denver. The original idea was to make a film called *U2 in the Americas*, featuring shows in both North and South America, but this was cancelled after logistical problems got in the way of a show in Argentina.

Musically the band were still exploring gospel and blues music. The new material on the album included 'Desire', 'Angel of Harlem' and 'When Love Comes to Town' – which all fared well when released as singles.

Of the live recordings on the album, they opened up with a cover of the Beatles' 'Helter Skelter' – mainly because the song symbolized the packed schedule of the *Joshua Tree* tour. A reworked version of 'I Still Haven't Found What I'm Looking For' complete with a gospel choir and a turbo-charged version of 'Bullet the Blue Sky' (which includes the lyric "rattle and hum") were the principal attractions.

With the *Rattle and Hum* double album being released less than 18 months after *The Joshua Tree*, the band were still at the stage where they could do no wrong. It went to Number 1 in most international charts and was generally seen as a live companion piece (with some new songs) to *The Joshua Tree* as opposed to being a new U2 album.

The film (also called *Rattle and Hum*) was released at the same time. Originally intended as an independent release for a niche market, the band's runaway success and commercial appeal saw it being given a full cinema release. While the film succeeds in capturing the U2 live experience, the band came across as over-earnest and grandiose. The critics weren't kind to the film, calling it misguided and bombastic.

It was a shock to the band to see themselves portrayed as Rock Gods on the big screen. As Bono would later tell the author: "Particularly back in Ireland where we were this post-punk band who were influenced by Joy Division and the Clash, the reaction back home [to the film *Rattle and Hum*] was that we had turned into a stadium-rock American showband. I mean, I was wearing a Stetson most of the time …"

> **"*Rattle and Hum* was conceived as a scrapbook, a memento of that time spent in America on the Joshua Tree tour. It changed when the movie, which was initially conceived as a low-budget film, suddenly became a big Hollywood affair."** The Edge

Significantly the tour that was used to promote the *Rattle and Hum* album – the Lovetown tour – avoided the US entirely, focusing instead on Australia/Japan and Europe. Creatively the band felt they were at a standstill; they were selling more albums than ever, but their new music seemed to be rooted in the past. In their darkest moments they felt that they had become the enemy – the gargantuan rock band that they had mocked when they were starting out as a New Wave band full of vim and vigour.

On one of the last Lovetown tour dates, a 1989 New Year's Eve show in Dublin, Bono sparked rumours that the band were breaking up when he announced at the end of the show: "This is the end of something for U2. We have to go away and dream it all up again."

At the beginning of the 1980s, U2 were still desperately looking for a recording contract. By the end of the decade they were musical superstars. But something was wrong. The world was changing around them (the Berlin Wall had fallen, apartheid was being dismantled) and the musical world was changing with dance music becoming the predominant means of expression. It was time to chop down the Joshua tree and start all over again.

OPPOSITE, TOP: On the way in to the 1988 Grammy Awards, where they won Best Album for *The Joshua Tree*.

OPPOSITE, BOTTOM: Bono in Paris in 1989 during the Lovetown tour.

ABOVE: The legendary guitarist B.B. King played on *Rattle and Hum* and joined the band on stage for some dates on the Lovetown tour.

RIGHT: Bono and Edge on stage in Paris for the Lovetown tour, 1989.

THE MAKING OF
ACHTUNG BABY (1991)

It was all change again as the band took the last-ever flight into East Berlin in October 1990 to get back in touch with their European musical roots on their new album. But this was a band in crisis, a real crisis.

While grateful for what *The Joshua Tree* and *Rattle and Hum* had given them in terms of commercial success, the band were running on empty at the end of the Lovetown tour. To move things forward they decided to go back to the music that had first inspired them. Discovering that key albums by David Bowie and Iggy Pop (both icons for U2) had been recorded in the famed Hansa studio in Berlin, the band travelled to the city on the eve of German reunification hoping that the tumultuous changes in the air would help with the musical changes they wanted on their new album.

The working title for their seventh studio album was *Man* – a play on the title of their first-ever release, *Boy*. Conditions weren't good: they weren't happy with their Berlin hotel, Hansa studio had fallen into disrepair and each band member had very different ideas of where they should be heading creatively.

The Edge had been embracing the new alternative rock scene and industrial music in particular; Bono was getting excited about hip-hop and the Madchester sound. On a personal level the band had been rocked by The Edge's crumbling marriage to his childhood sweetheart

– U2 was always a very tight band in terms of their relationships and this was the first crack in their set-up.

Tensions were escalated by Bono and The Edge writing as a duo and not involving Larry and Adam in the process. Larry was beginning to feel marginalized by the suggestion they use drum machines on the new album, thus reducing his role.

There were two opposing camps in the studio: on one side Bono and Edge arguing for a club culture/dance music influence on the new songs – Bono had always been dismayed by the fact that whenever he was out in a club and a U2 record came on, it would empty the dance floor. In the other corner were producer Daniel Lanois and Larry and Adam. While they admired the ideas Bono and Edge had, they just didn't hear any songs coming from their musical sketches.

Things deteriorated so badly that at one stage Bono and Daniel Lanois almost came to blows during the recording of the 'Mysterious Ways' song. For the first time U2 had reached a personal and professional impasse. Berlin had become a nightmare as band members lost trust in each other.

Bono and Edge announced that they wanted "to chop down the Joshua tree". They wanted a sexy new European sound, complete with dance rhythms to kill off the Stetson-hat-wearing, stadium-rock Gods that U2 had become in the late 1980s. But Larry and Adam felt that, while they were talking a good album, they had nothing concrete to show.

Speaking to the author years later, Bono confessed that the situation in the recording studio in Berlin had actually been far worse than they ever admitted at the time, saying, "On a scale of one to ten, we were at a nine for breaking up."

One night in the studio, The Edge was playing around with a discarded second bridge section from a song called 'Sick Puppy' (later renamed 'Mysterious Ways'). There was something special in this chord progression and the band soon picked up on it. Collaboratively, a whole song emerged within 15 minutes. The lyrics Bono had for it were all about the tension between band members at the time and the contrast with the political reunification happening outside the studio's doors. They called the song 'One'.

The Edge remembers the moment as if "suddenly something very powerful was happening in the room"; while Bono recalls, "As soon as 'One' came into that room in Hansa, it stabilized everything. Everyone just sort of surrendered after we had that. By surrendering, we got over the hump."

Exhausted but relieved, the band returned home to Dublin for Christmas. They might have an album after all.

OPPOSITE: "The Fly" was a leather-clad egomaniac created by Bono for the album *Achtung Baby* as a parody of rock stardom. Here he is on stage in Rotterdam, July 1992.

ABOVE LEFT: Bono walks among the audience during a show at New York's Madison Square Gardens in 1991.

ABOVE RIGHT: On the Zoo TV tour, Bono sent up his old, sanctimonious image, replacing it with a new playfulness.

ACHTUNG BABY

(1991)

Back in Dublin, the band held a series of meetings. There was still fall-out from the Berlin sessions, but all were committed to the new album, no matter where it would take them.

Berlin had seen U2 coming apart slowly and it was only the glimmer of hope provided by 'One' that convinced the band to continue with what they had started. After a six-week break, they decided to rent a house near to where Bono and The Edge lived in Dublin and complete the album from there.

Nerves were frayed in Berlin, and now a more careful listen back to what they had recorded in Hansa studios showed that there was some very good material there. With the band functioning again as a unit, the songs began to take shape. What the Hansa experience had taught them was that they could work through even seemingly insurmountable problems and this allowed the band to believe in the old adage of what doesn't kill you, makes you stronger.

To distance himself from his serious and over-earnest frontman image, Bono decided to come up with an over-the-top character which

he called "The Fly" – named after the song in which the character first appeared. Wearing ridiculously big black sunglasses and dressed in rock star leather, The Fly was a caricature of an ego-obsessed rock frontman.

Lyrically they dispensed with the anthemic socio-political approach of *The Joshua Tree* and instead rooted these songs in broken relationships, love / sexuality and darker themes such as betrayal and inter-personal discord.

Three songs in particular, 'Ultraviolet (Light My Way)', 'Love is Blindness' and 'Who's Gonna Ride Your Wild Horses', dealt with the breakdown of a relationship and its repercussions.

Musically, they had indeed cut down the Joshua tree. Gone were the primary colours of bass, guitar and drum, to be replaced by songs that were progressive and forward-looking. 'Mysterious Ways' and 'Even Better Than the Real Thing' in particular introduced a more club-culture sound, and dance remixes of these tracks actually put U2 on the dance floor for the first time in their career.

Simultaneously, the band had dropped the po-faced seriousness and search for musical meaning that so weighed down *Rattle and Hum* and were now being playful, ironic and flippant.

Even the album's cover art work – a collage of photos taken in Berlin, Spain and Morocco, including a naked shot of Adam Clayton – was worlds apart from the stern-looking men on *The Joshua Tree*. The album's title was changed from *Man* to *Achtung Baby* after the band heard their sound engineer, Joe O'Herlihy, using the phrase during recording.

But this was U2's "heaviest" album – as Bono described it. Personal, upfront and speaking of the turmoil of its creation, these lyrics didn't look outside to the world but inside to the damaged heart and soul. To give this very different-sounding album a chance to breathe, the band did minimal promotion and no advance copies were made available to the press; the idea was that listeners were given time to assimilate the new sound.

The album took a while to get going commercially, but it remains one of the band's biggest sellers. Critically, it was fawned over – particularly by those who found *Rattle and Hum* hard to take. The third single off the album – 'One', the song that had saved them in Berlin – has gone on to become one of their best-known tracks.

The album was only half the story of U2's reinvention for the 1990s. They were already planning a very different type of tour. Traditionally the band had used austere-looking stage sets, but for *Achtung Baby* they wanted to throw anything and everything at the stage. The break with the past would be complete.

But the real triumph of *Achtung Baby* – and it's still U2's favourite album – lies in the fact that it shows the band could move with the times; they could "dream it all up again" as Bono had promised from the stage of their New Year's Eve show in Dublin. This was a band who were built for longevity.

U2's second chapter had got off to an interesting start.

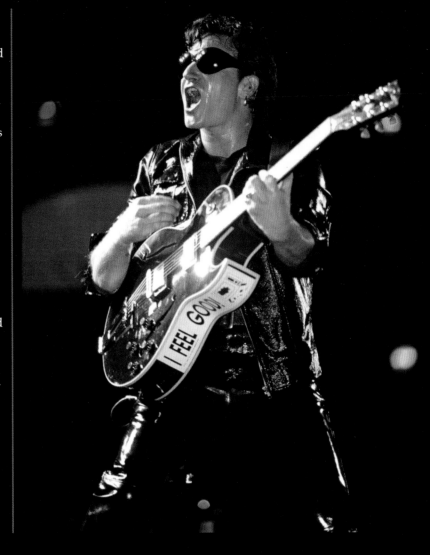

> **"Making *Achtung Baby* is the reason why we're still here now."** Bono

Opposite: Zoo TV was a tour that rewrote the rulebook for live rock music. Note the Trabant car hanging from the lighting system.

Top: According to Bono, *Achtung Baby* and the Zoo TV tour were "the sound of four men chopping down the Joshua Tree".

Far Left: Also appearing on the Zoo TV tour was the lounge lizard "MacPhisto".

Left: Bono and Adam at McNichols Arena in Denver, Colorado in April 1987.

LARRY MULLEN JR

Larry Mullen is the quiet one in U2. Not a fan of the celebrity lifestyle, he is the anchor of the band and an outstanding drummer in his own right.

Laurence Joseph Mullen was born on 31 October 1961. Long since known as Larry, he added the "Jr" to his name only when U2 started making money and his father (who has the same name) started getting his tax bills.

Originally a piano student, he was on his way out of a lesson in a Dublin music school when he heard someone clattering the drums in another room. Persuading his parents to allow him to switch classes, he soon discovered a natural gift for percussion. Continually practising by himself at home bored him, so his father advised him to put up a note at school looking for other musicians to play with.

At the time of the first U2 audition in Larry's kitchen he was just 14, but he was the only trained musician in the band. It was also supposed to be the Larry Mullen Band since it was his idea and, unlike the others, he could actually play. However, within ten minutes of Bono arriving, the dynamic changed.

In the early days of U2, Larry and Bono were very close – they were the only two Irish-born members of U2 and came from similar working family backgrounds. They both endured the trauma of losing their mothers when they were teenagers. Larry, as with Bono, believes it was the grief of his mother's early death which led him to form a rock band.

Larry's father was never entirely happy about his young son throwing in his lot with a rock band which didn't exactly display any promise in the early days. So the drummer was the only U2 member to have a day job, and Larry actually missed a lot of the early U2 photo shoots and gigs because of his work (his place was always taken by a stand-in).

With Bono and The Edge, Larry joined the Shalom Christian group while still at school. Just like the others, however, he left when a choice had to be made between his faith and his commitment to a touring rock band.

He is a very underestimated drummer: long-time U2 producer Brian Eno tells a story about how when recording the *All You Can't Leave Behind* album, the drummer felt that the click track (a computer-generated beat) was out of time. Eno assured him it wasn't but Larry kept arguing it was. It was only later that Eno realized that the click track was two milliseconds out of time. Eno believes Larry's drumming and precise sense of timing is "staggering".

Combining a number of styles – from his militaristic-style drumming on the *War* album to the more electronic syncopated approach on the *Pop* album – his drum loops have been the basis of many a U2 song.

The only member of the band to remain living on the north side of Dublin (where all of U2 grew up), Larry is the least comfortable with the celebrity status of being in a rock band. His best friends are those he has known most of his adult life and he never courts media attention. He is at his happiest when riding his beloved Harley-Davidson – often using it for transport between shows in different cities.

Within the group, Larry is regarded as being the voice of reason. When the songs aren't working and too much indulgent experimentalism is seeping in, he will be the first to pull the band back to the core of a song.

His relationship with Bono is complex. While he unreservedly supports the singer's activist work, he is concerned about how much studio time Bono misses because of his outside commitments. He is uncomfortable with some of Bono's political acquaintances.

Outside of U2, he has produced albums by many an emerging Irish rock band, and he has also worked with artists such as Nanci Griffith, Robbie Robertson and Emmylou Harris. He and Adam Clayton were briefly members of a supergroup with R.E.M.'s Michael Stipe and Mike Mills called Automatic Baby. Alongside Adam Clayton, he worked on the theme music song to the *Mission: Impossible* film.

Larry has been with his girlfriend, Anne Acheson, for over 30 years – they first met at the same Dublin school. They have three children but avoid the limelight. Over the last few years he has begun an acting career. In 2011 he acted alongside Donald Sutherland in *Man on the Train* and two years later he appeared with Juliette Binoche in *A Thousand Times Goodnight*.

His main passions outside of U2 are the Irish football team and Elvis Presley.

LEFT: The engine room of U2 – Larry Mullen Jr at work on the Joshua Tree tour.
OPPOSITE (CLOCKWISE FROM TOP LEFT): U2 were first called "The Larry Mullen Band" because it was the drummer who initially got the band together; a very youthful Larry in Dublin in 1977; long-time U2 producer, Brian Eno, refers to Mullen as "a drumming genius"; the most down-to-earth member of the band, Larry has, as Bono puts it, "saved us from ourselves, many a time".

U2 REINVENT TOURING

Lights, camera and sensory overload action. The Zoo TV tour rewrote the rulebook for the live music tour. ABBA, Trabant cars and an order for 10,000 pizzas were bonus features.

The Zoo TV tour ran for two years, 1992–1993, but such was its scale and scope that intense planning for it had begun months before *Achtung Baby* was released. For The Edge, it was a thrilling adventure for the band to "smash U2 up and start all over again". Everything was up for grabs; the only ideas that were ruled out were anything to do with U2 in the 1980s – Stetson hats, white flags and over-earnestness.

The band wanted to reflect the "new Europe" in their stage set-up (with the Berlin Wall gone, Europe was busy reshaping itself) and also wanted an acknowledgement of how crucial their time in Berlin was to the *Achtung Baby* album. While in Berlin, they had been watching coverage of the First Gulf War on television and were struck by how images of death and destruction were interrupted by ad breaks – the agony of war side by side with the crassness of consumerism.

Technology was advancing rapidly in the early 1990s and the show would also nod to the emerging new media. Zoo TV would feature video banks and pre-recorded film material to add to the feeling of "sensory bombardment" and audio-visual excess.

While in Berlin the band had formed a bizarre attachment to the Trabant car – for many the symbol of East Germany and the wall coming down. The idea was to buy up as many old Trabants as they could, fit them out with lighting systems and hang them from the ceilings during shows. As the band went on a shopping spree for the Zoo TV stage, the costs mounted – but it was all or nothing for the band at this stage. Live television transmissions, Bono making live prank phone calls from the stage and a "confession box" for audience members were all added to the mix.

The first two legs of Zoo TV (in the US and Europe) were indoors and featured a "B" stage – a smaller platform off the main stage used by the band for more acoustic-style numbers. To adequately capture the new songs live, the band seriously considered bringing in other musicians, but ultimately they were reluctant to do away with the classic four-piece lineup, so some pre-recorded backing music was used instead.

The show was spectacular and despite some hardcore U2 fans being confused by this very different band doing a very different live show, the critics agreed that live rock music was being presented in an exciting and dynamic new way. Nearly all the tour shows opened with either six or eight *Achtung Baby* songs before the band even thought about using any back catalogue material.

Bono was in character throughout – either as "The Fly", "Mirror Ball Man" or "MacPhisto" – all of them grotesque but humorous rock star caricatures. "I became this identikit rock star, an assemble-it-yourself rock star, it was incredibly freeing. The characters could say things I couldn't," he said of his nightly transformation. The preaching

and flag-waving of previous tours had been replaced by a multi-media circus in fancy dress and such was the visual assault of the show that demand for tickets was soon outstripping supply.

There was fun – members of ABBA joining the band in Stockholm for a version of 'Dancing Queen' – intermixed with serious matters – the band conducted live satellite link-ups with people in Sarajevo during the Bosnian war to hear about the trauma visited on the city.

As successful as Zoo TV was, it leaked money at every turn. U2 saw the huge costs of their travelling carnival as an investment – not a financial one but a musical one for their future wellbeing. But the margins were so slim that Bono was to later reveal: "When we built Zoo TV we were so close to bankruptcy that if five per cent fewer people went (to the shows), U2 was bankrupt. It was terrifying."

Manager Paul McGuinness put it more bluntly: "We grossed $30 million in T-shirt sales. Without those we'd be fucked."

The second two legs of Zoo TV went outdoors in the US and Europe. By the time the tour finished up with a final set of shows in Australia and Japan at the end of 1993, the tour had been seen by well over five million people. In between all the madness, there had been time for a new album.

OPPOSITE, TOP: For their Zoo TV tour in the early 1990s, the band overhauled not only their music but also how they looked.

OPPOSITE, BOTTOM: Bono in his treasured gold lamé suit from the tour – here in the guise of the shady underworld figure of "MacPhisto".

TOP: With its banks of video screens, Zoo TV was the precursor of the stadium rock show as we know it now.

RIGHT: Lasting two years, the Zoo TV tour remains the band's crowning artistic achievement. And *Achtung Baby* remains the band's favourite album.

ZOOROPA

(1993)

With Zoo TV exceeding all expectations, the band were on a creative roll. With a few months off between tour dates, they produced the quickest-ever-recorded U2 album.

There were six months off between the outdoor legs of the US and Europe Zoo TV tour in 1993, and given the high levels of energy and excitement being felt by the tour, the band immediately set about recoding an EP that would be out in time for the European dates. There was plenty of material – there were still unfinished songs from the *Achtung Baby* sessions that just needed knocking into shape and the soundchecks for the tour dates also yielded some promising new material.

For Bono, the "madness" of the Zoo TV tour was about to spill over into the "madness" of the *Zooropa* album. The EP idea was soon ditched as the band realized they had an album and the race was on to have it out before the tour resumed in May 1993.

The *Zooropa* songs were directly inspired by the tour and continued in the same vein as *Achtung Baby*, albeit with an even more experimental, futuristic sound. The title track used lyrics direct from advertising slogans and imagined a cyberpunk city. The first single off the album, 'Numb', was a U2 first – The Edge on lead vocals singing a series of commands in a monotone voice.

With sound effects and samples used throughout, the album had an other-worldly feel and was synthesizer-heavy. With no real time to agonize over the songs, this was very much a tour soundtrack album. Technology and the numbing effects of mass media – core themes of the tour – were still very much ideas to be played around with on the songs.

On 'Lemon' – inspired by some old video footage Bono had received of his late mother wearing a lemon dress – the band produced a distorted disco song marked by falsetto vocals, while on 'Stay (Faraway, So Close!)' – probably the most traditional U2 song on the album – they delved into the area of domestic violence. While Johnny Cash was visiting Dublin, the band got him in to record the vocals on the album's closing track – 'The Wanderer'. Bono always maintained it was Cash's voice he heard during the writing of the song.

These months off from the tour proved to be the most productive time the band had ever had in the studio. Instead of decompressing and returning to normal life, they just kept going, knowing they were on a deadline. When Zoo TV resumed in May of that year, the album wasn't quite finished but the band were so charged up that they took the decision to fly home to Dublin each night after the European dates so they could complete the work and have it out in time for the last few months of the tour.

It was an insane schedule, but they got the album in the shops in early July. For the remaining 30 Zoo TV tour dates, songs from *Zooropa* featured heavily. Now viewed more as a coda to *Achtung Baby*, the album was about as spontaneous as the band would ever get. Although enthused by it at the time of release, the band have come over time to regard it with mixed feelings. Commercially it sold well on the back of the tour, but it didn't have anywhere near the chart longevity of its parent album – *Achtung Baby*.

The *Zooropa* sessions also, without the band knowing it at the time, represented the beginning of their 1997 *Pop* album – four unreleased

Zooropa songs made it on to the *Pop* album. But before all that there was time, post-Zoo TV tour, to take another creative swerve. The side project album *Original Soundtracks Volume 1* – released in 1995 and credited to Passengers (who were U2 and Brian Eno) – is the U2 album everyone forgets about.

The idea was to write soundtrack songs for films that didn't exist. With that in mind, and still very much in experimental mode, the band wrote a series of visual songs that were mainly instrumental or featured disconnected vocals. The album did throw up one song, though, which many regard as their finest hour – the haunting 'Miss Sarajevo' – the only song from *Original Soundtracks* ever to be played live.

Because it went out under a different name, the album isn't viewed as being part of the U2 canon. But it did have an important role to play – it marked the winding down of the *Achtung Baby* / Zoo TV years – and when the band next resurfaced they promised the album of their careers.

| **"*Zooropa* was a good plan; but it almost killed us."** Bono

OPPOSITE, LEFT: Bono and Adam Clayton on the Zoo TV tour in Rotterdam, May 1993.
OPPOSITE, RIGHT: These particular sunglasses were originally given to Bono in the studio while making *Achtung Baby*, to lighten the mood of sometimes fraught recording sessions.
LEFT: The Trabant cars hanging from the ceiling weren't simply for decoration on the Zoo TV tour – they contained the lighting system.
BELOW: The dollar bills on the floor around Bono's feet were thrown there each night during a barnstorming version of 'Bullet the Blue Sky'.

POP

(1997)

Towards the end of a triumphant decade, U2 promised the be-all and end-all of albums with _Pop_. But with an injured drummer and a tour already booked, their best-laid plans went awry.

The album that was supposed to be U2's crowning glory was recorded over two years with a revolving cast of producers. _Pop_ was to be the follow-up to the career-reviving _Achtung Baby_ and the band certainly felt they were in the right place to produce the album of their lives. A full-on dance music album was expected by many given that regular producers Brian Eno and Daniel Lanois sat this album out and instead the job was given to leading dance music figures Howie B. and Steve Osborne, with Flood also making a major contribution.

The band were eager to push on from the _Achtung Baby_ sound but wanted to retain that album's flirtation with the dance music scene but in a more focused way. The Edge prepared audiences for a dance album when he said of the early recordings "the thinking was that we were going to further experiment … accepting the influence and aesthetics of dance music".

Larry Mullen was absent from the first album sessions due to having surgery on a long-standing back injury and the band played around with drum loops in his absence. Mullen, knowing that the outline of each U2 album is formulated during these early sessions, wasn't happy the band continued without him.

Using more sequencing and sampling effects than ever before and with The Edge's guitar sound bent out of all recognizable shape, the band did struggle to get on top of how the new material was going to be presented and songs were mixed and remixed to within an inch of their lives.

When the album eventually emerged in March 1997, Bono summed it up neatly by saying, "It begins at a party and ends at a funeral." The first three tracks – 'Discotheque', 'Do You Feel Loved' and 'Mofo' – were electronic assaults before they returned to their more traditional sound with 'If God Will Send His Angels', 'Staring at the Sun' and 'Last Night on Earth'. The pace of the album slows down considerably over the last few tracks with the songs being more reminiscent of the _Original Soundtracks Volume 1_ album.

With so many producers coming and going on re-mix duties, the band found it hard to settle on any particular arrangement for any of the songs and then made the fatal mistake of allowing the accompanying PopMart tour to be booked for April 1997.

Pop was scheduled for release in November 1996 to allow the band rehearsal time for the tour, but the deadline was missed as the band went into their now customary last-minute dash to complete the album. The album was eventually released just six weeks before the tour started. They still felt it was only half-finished, but their hands were tied by the upcoming world tour.

Pop sold very well in its first few weeks but then soon trailed off. Its sales are among the lowest of any U2 albums (over their whole career), becoming the band's first wrong move in the 1990s. It still remains a contentious album for band members – they feel there was a masterpiece in there somewhere, but what they put out was rush-released to meet the tour and didn't reflect what had gone down in the studio.

The early dates of the PopMart tour suffered from the lack of rehearsal time. It was an over-the-top stage production featuring a gigantic LED screen, a 30-metre (100ft) high golden arch and a large

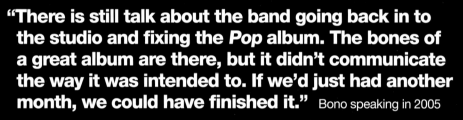

"There is still talk about the band going back in to the studio and fixing the *Pop* album. The bones of a great album are there, but it didn't communicate the way it was intended to. If we'd just had another month, we could have finished it." Bono speaking in 2005

mirror-ball lemon. A commentary on consumerism, the PopMart production had lofty ideals but left many wondering where the actual band was amid all the hi-tech sound, lights and props.

There were, though, two big highlights: the band fulfilled a promise to the people of Sarajevo to play in their city (after the Zoo TV tour had featured their plight extensively) and their performance remains a treasured band memory. The tour also went to South America (a first for the band) and the rapturous reception they received there reinvigorated them as a band.

U2 had simply got their timing wrong with the album and the tour. The *Pop* album was changing dramatically in sound and structure from month to month and if they had been given some extra time, the album could have gelled properly. It is rare now to hear any of the *Pop* songs on U2 tours – a sure sign the band felt they didn't realize their potential with it.

It was time now to dispense with the garish stage clothes, the circus-like stage productions and move back from the electronic experimentalism. When U2 next re-emerged, it was back to basics. But with a twist.

OPPOSITE, LEFT: The extravagant PopMart tour opened in Las Vegas in April 1997. Early reviews were mixed, some critics confused by the band's attempt to satirize consumerist culture.

OPPOSITE, RIGHT: PopMart's centrepiece was a Golden Arch 30 metre (100 feet) high.

TOP LEFT: Adam Clayton with mouth guard and industrial wear at a PopMart show in Oakland, California in June 1997.

TOP RIGHT: Bono with his treasured red guitar when PopMart hit Rotterdam in 1997.

RIGHT: The Edge, dressed as an urban cowboy, with his trusty Rickenbacker in Rotterdam.

ALL THAT YOU CAN'T LEAVE BEHIND (2000)

The party was over. U2 had enjoyed the fun-fair that was Zoo TV and PopMart in the 1990s, but as a new decade dawned they wanted to be a four-piece rock band again.

Neither the *Pop* album nor the PopMart tour had truly met expectations. For once, U2 seemed to be treading water and clutching at experimental straws. The *Pop* album hadn't sold as well as predicted and the main complaint about the trashy extravagance of the PopMart tour was that the four band members seemed to get lost amid all the stage props and technological bells and whistles.

If, in a sense, U2 spent the 1990s trying their best not to sound like U2, for the new decade they decided it was time to try to sound more like the band they once were again. Long-time producers Brian Eno and Daniel Lanois were brought back in to produce the new album and Eno was keen for the band to get back into the studio as soon as possible after the PopMart tour – sensing that too much time off would only give the band the chance to worry about possible new directions.

Gathering together in Dublin just months after the lights were switched off on PopMart, the band all agreed (quite a rare thing with four different individuals in the group) that they would return to a bass, guitar, drums sound and that the best way to facilitate this was for the four of them to write and record together in a small room. A lot like they had done for the first three U2 albums.

The first song to arrive for the album that had the working title *U2000* was 'Kite'. This was a crucial moment because the vocal was demanding, but Bono nailed the high notes. His full vocal range was back again.

'Beautiful Day', which was the important first single release off the album, threw up an interesting – and contradictory – band discussion. The guitar sounds The Edge put on the song were reminiscent of his work in the early 1980s and the other band members wanted a more forward-looking sound. The Edge won the argument and 'Beautiful Day' remains a key song for the band – being the only song (apart from 'One' and 'Vertigo') to feature in every single U2 concert since it was introduced.

Although the album side-stepped most of their 1990s experimental electronic textures, it wasn't a retro-sounding affair. The tight melody lines of the album did hark back to *The Joshua Tree*, but sonically it incorporated the technological advances that the modern recording studio now allowed.

The album's second single 'Stuck In a Moment You Can't Get Out Of' was written about the death of Bono's good friend, the INXS singer Michael Hutchence, while 'Walk On' was written as a result of the band being awarded the Freedom of the City of Dublin in 2000. Also receiving the same accolade that year was the Burmese academic Aung San Suu Kyi, who had been fighting for full democracy in her homeland. Never having heard of the woman before the Dublin award, the band researched her plight and came up with 'Walk On' in her honour.

> **"I think on the last album, *Pop*, we had obliterated the band, it all became too abstract. On this one we just decided 'Here are the songs' and we found ourselves using sounds that we hadn't used since *Boy*. It's a simple album, but the challenge was to make something simple mean a lot."** The Edge

All That You Can't Leave Behind was released in October 2000. It went on to sell 12 million copies and pick up seven Grammy Awards. Noting that it was a radical departure from their 1990s work, critics realized this wasn't U2 going backwards but rather a band acknowledging their own past with one eye on the future. Tellingly the album's sleeve featured a black-and-white shot of the band – all the 1990s albums were in colour.

The accompanying Elevation tour, which ran throughout 2001, saw the band avoiding stadia, opting instead to play more intimate-style arena shows which featured a relatively sparse stage design. The tour was one of the band's happiest and most hassle-free but was challenging for Bono because his father was dying of cancer at the time; during the European dates he would fly back to Dublin each night to spend the night in the hospital with him. The third leg of the tour (beginning in October 2001) saw the band do their first shows in the US since the calamitous events of 9/11. The band still regard their two shows in New York's Madison Square Gardens from that time as two of their most memorable shows.

One notable feature of the recording of *All That You Can't Leave Behind* is that Bono was absent from a lot of the recordings. He had just got involved with a grouping called Jubilee 2000, which was calling for the cancellation of Third World debt. He was spending more and more of his time now as an activist …

OPPOSITE, TOP: To promote *All That You Can't Leave Behind*, released in 2000, the band played an impromptu show in Times Square, New York.
OPPOSITE BELOW: The band on their way into the NME Carling Awards, in London 2002, to receive the award for Best Live Act.
BELOW: Bono pictured at one of U2's smallest-ever shows – when they played to 2,000 people at London's Astoria Theatre in February 2001 ahead of their Elevation tour.

BONO THE ACTIVIST

From the White House to G8 Summits, Bono has had an Access All Areas backstage pass to argue his case for economic justice for Africa. But his activism has caused strains within U2.

Whether it's to do with his teenage membership of a Christian prayer group, his sense of curiosity and adventure or the fact that his privileged lifestyle allows him to get involved in philanthropic works, Bono has becoming a leading activist for causes relating to the African continent. It helps that his celebrity status opens doors for him and attracts the media to report on his work. It doesn't help – from his bandmates' point of view – that his commitment to his activism has at times reduced his role within U2.

Visiting Ethiopia with his wife, Ali, for six weeks after the Live Aid concert of 1985 sparked an attachment to the continent and a resolution to help, however he could. Bono primarily argues that the debt owed by African countries needs to be restructured to encourage their economic growth and that the developed world needs to work harder to help prevent the spread of HIV/AIDS on the continent.

His advocacy work has seen him nominated three times for the Nobel Peace Prize and awarded a knighthood in the British honour lists in 2007. His early work at the end of the 1990s with Jubilee 2000, a lobby group calling for the cancellation of all debt owed by developing countries, led to work with the ONE campaign and the DATA group – both of which called for economic equality for African countries, the adjusting of international trade rules which militate against African countries and the elimination of curable diseases on the continent.

His work with these various groupings leads him to meet political leaders worldwide to argue his case and visit African countries to see for himself what is being done. These commitments sometimes clash with U2 recording sessions and although the rest of the band are supportive of his efforts, they do have concerns about how much time and energy he has left for U2.

His activist work is not without controversy. When he informed The Edge that he was meeting with President Bush in 2005 to discuss debt relief for Africa and there would be pictures of them together on the White House lawn shaking hands and smiling, The Edge tried to talk him out of the photo session, but to no avail. The Edge was anxious about U2 being seen to endorse a particular political leader.

Bono's friendship with Britain's ex-Prime Minister Tony Blair (Bono has spoken at a Labour Party conference) does not sit easily with Larry Mullen. While Mullen does acknowledge that Bono "is prepared to use his weight as a celebrity at great cost to himself to help other people", the drummer has said he "cringes" when he sees the singer with Tony Blair and George Bush. Mullen regards both Bush and Blair as "war criminals".

Not known for doing anything by the half-measure, Bono is aware of the absurdity of a multi-millionaire rock star preaching about Third World debt and poverty but takes his commitment seriously. He prides himself on the fact that he can talk for more than an hour on HIPC conditionality – the terms under which the most highly indebted countries of the world are forgiven their loans – and has taken crash courses in economics, sociology and political theory so that he knows what he is talking about during meetings with the world's most influential political leaders.

"I've met people the band would rather I didn't meet," Bono has said of his activist work. "And there are some people I have to talk to, or appear in a photograph with, that in other circumstances I'd rather not."

Closer to home, it was Bono's idea to get two Northern Irish political leaders representing both sides of the divide to shake hands on stage at a show in Belfast just before a crucial referendum in 1998 about the political future of the country.

In 1999 Bono had an audience with the Pope to discuss Third World poverty. Noticing the Pope was interested in his trademark "Fly" sunglasses, the singer offered them to the pontiff, who promptly tried them on for size. The Vatican press office has never made the ensuing photograph available to the public.

Bono's main work now is with his PRODUCT(RED) campaign. Set up to encourage large companies who sell global brands to mark some of their range with the PRODUCT(RED) logo and to donate a percentage of the profit to benefit HIV/AIDS relief in Africa, the campaign has secured backing from many leading brands.

Pictured on the cover of *Time* magazine in 2002 for his activist work, the headline read: "Can Bono Save the World?". To his friends back in Dublin this was changed to "Can the World be Saved from Bono?"

OPPOSITE, LEFT: In Mali in 2012, Bono meets Soumana Kotota and her children. The singer was in Mali to highlight the country's drive to reduce malnutrition levels.
OPPOSITE, RIGHT: Bono spent New Year's Eve 1995 in the war-torn city of Sarajevo. During the Zoo TV tour, the singer conducted regular live linkups to people in the city to hear how the civil war was destroying lives.
RIGHT: Bono with Nelson Mandela, his all-time hero, in 2000.
BOTTOM LEFT: In the White House Oval Office with President Barack Obama to discuss international aid policy in April 2010.
BOTTOM RIGHT: As an activist, Bono is called upon to give almost as many speeches as he plays live shows.

> "Hanging out with politicians and corporations is very unhip work. The band thought this [his activist work] would sink the ship ten years ago. I am not an idealist, never have been. I am just quite pragmatic about finding solutions. Preventing fires is cheaper than putting them out." Bono

HOW TO DISMANTLE AN ATOMIC BOMB (2004)

One of their best-ever singles, an album that couldn't stop selling, an Apple iPod tie-in and one of their best-ever tours. U2 had reached another new high-water mark.

Early indications that the follow-up to *All That You Can't Leave Behind* would be a continuation of the band's route one rock music approach were confirmed when it was announced that Steve Lillywhite was back on production duties and that Bono was getting himself into the right songwriting frame of mind by going back and listening to the bands who first inspired him – the Buzzcocks and Siouxsie and the Banshees in particular.

Buoyed up by the fact that they were allowed – from both a commercial and critical perspective – to revisit their past and strip things back down to their core strengths on *All That You Can't Leave Behind*, the band now decided to produce a full-on rock album – loaded with riffs and melodies.

The opening single from the clumsily titled *How to Dismantle an Atomic Bomb* said a lot about where the band were at the time of recording. 'Vertigo' begins with Bono saying "Uno, dos, tres, catorce" – Spanish for "One, two, three, fourteen". This was a reference to Steve Lillywhite who, having produced U2's first three albums, was now back producing their fourteenth album (counting compilations). Shortly afterwards, on 'Vertigo', Bono is heard saying off-mike "Turn it up, Captain." This is a reference to Nick Stewart (whom Bono nicknamed "the captain"). It was Stewart who issued U2 with their first recording contract with Island Records back in 1980 (the contract was signed in the ladies' toilets at the Lyceum Theatre in London).

'Sometimes You Can't Make It on Your Own' was written about Bono's late father, Bob Hewson – it hadn't always been the easiest of relationships with two headstrong male members of the same family, but the singer felt his father's death keenly. Bono would be frequently moved to tears performing this song live.

'City of Blinding Lights' and 'All Because of You' continued the rock 'n' roll momentum and the band were thrilled to find that when *How to Dismantle an Atomic Bomb* was released on 22 November 2004, it went straight to Number 1 in 32 countries worldwide.

The band entered into an agreement with the Apple company, which saw 'Vertigo' being used as a widely viewed advertisement for the Apple iPod. No money changed hands in the deal; U2 agreed to promote the iPod only because they believed that music was beginning to suffer from illegal downloading of songs and iTunes seemed to them to represent the best legal and fair alternative to purchase music. Special edition U2 iPods were also made available as part of the tie-in.

The 'Vertigo' iPod ad brought the band to a whole new generation of fans. It caused no end of amusement to the band when newer fans would tell them "We go all the way back to the early albums such as *Achtung Baby*."

To put the album's Grammy Award-winning status in context: Michael Jackson's *Thriller* won eight Grammys; *How to Dismantle an*

> "I'd like to think this is a real classic U2 album and that there is this spine to it. I have a feeling that looking back on this album in a few years' time it will have a very strong identity from beginning to end and ultimately that's what an album is about."
>
> The Edge

Atomic Bomb won nine. U2 still share the record for the most Grammys awarded to a single album with Santana's *Supernatural* album.

The Vertigo tour was even more successful than the album. Selling close to five million tickets over 131 shows (the majority of them sell-outs), it became the second-highest-grossing tour ever at the time. Featuring songs from their debut *Boy* album as well as almost every other album, the tour's setlist was their most career-spanning ever.

The encore featured a mini version of Zoo TV with 'Zoo Station', 'The Fly' and 'Mysterious Ways' all featuring. A lot of shows had '40' as their last-ever song – reminiscent of how they used to close the War tour from 22 years earlier in their career.

As some measure of how happy the band were with the tour, three concert films were released (in place of the usual one): *Vertigo 2005: Live from Chicago*, *Vertigo: Live from Milan* and a *U2 Live in 3D* concert film.

The year 2005 will perhaps remain U2's most successful ever. A global Number 1 for their album, one of the fastest-selling and biggest-grossing live tours of all time and a whole new generation of fans who heard them first through the 'Vertigo' single.

Twenty-five years into their career and U2 were beginning to lighten up and relax. They were reconciled with their music past, thrilled with their record-breaking present and excited about what lay ahead. But does anything ever go as planned in U2's world?

OPPOSITE, TOP: Bono singing 'Vertigo' – the lead-off single from 2004's *How to Dismantle an Atomic Bomb*.

OPPOSITE, BOTTOM: Bono and Edge harmonizing – their voices have blended better as the years have gone by.

TOP: Rehearsing for the Elevation tour in Dublin in 2004.

LEFT: The band staged a free gig outdoors in New York City on 22 November 2004, to mark the release of *How to Dismantle an Atomic Bomb*.

NO LINE ON THE HORIZON (2009)

There was trouble from the start; a scrapped album session, no notable single and a confusion of sounds led to a troubled album. But the tour was quite another matter.

There was a more than five-year wait for *No Line on the Horizon* – the longest ever delay between U2 albums. Three years previous to its release the band had been in the studio with the noted producer Rick Rubin, but that material was never used. Instead U2 started again and took the unusual step of having someone other than themselves working on the songs – both Brian Eno and Daniel Lanois got songwriting credits on the album.

It was clear the band weren't quite sure what they had in mind. When they began recording they believed they were going to release two EPs – one called 'Daylight', the other 'Darkness' – but instead they combined the tracks for a full album.

No Line on the Horizon began with a trip to Morocco, and their intention then was to put out an album which was as different to *How to Dismantle an Atomic Bomb* as *Achtung Baby* had been to *The Joshua Tree*. But when they returned to Dublin they found that these World Music-influenced tracks just weren't the sound of the band and would be impossible to play live.

Musically the album was a combination of styles from rock to folk to songs infused with ethnic and gospel influences. Lyrically Bono began writing in the third person, inventing a number of characters to tell the songs' stories. With tracks running to six and seven minutes long, it was a very different-sounding album. With 'Moment of

Surrender' and 'Unknown Caller' they did break new ground, but the album suffered from a lack of a big, first single.

'Get On Your Boots' was one of the band's quickest-ever songs in terms of tempo, and its electro-grunge appeal just didn't sit with the more reflective tones of the album. As a single, it was five musical ideas compressed into one and commercially it became the band's first lead-off single not to enter the UK Top 10 singles chart since 1981.

The lack of one stand-out song did impact on the album's profile and chart performance. Whereas the previous album, *How to Dismantle an Atomic Bomb,* had five singles released, only three singles were released from *No Line on the Horizon.* The second single, 'Magnificent', didn't break the UK Top 40 while the third single 'I'll Go Crazy if I Don't Go Crazy Tonight' didn't get into the UK Top 30.

The album sales were disappointing – it struggled to hit the one million sales mark in the US. The band were shaken by how relatively poorly it sold but an ambitious tour, the 360° tour, was consuming all their time. It featured a massive, space-age, four-legged structure which became known as "The Claw", and the band performed under it. This particular configuration enabled the band to play in the round – meaning the audience surrounded the stage.

Running from June 2009 to July 2011, the tour sold out in record time. Featuring live linkups to the International Space Station and their entire 2009 Pasadena California show being broadcast live on YouTube, the tour was well received with many noting that the atypical stage configuration – U2 were effectively playing in the middle of stadia – allowed the band to be more visible than they had ever been live. It's the only U2 tour to feature songs from every one of their albums – including *October.* They stepped out of 360° "The Claw" mode only once during the tour – to perform at 2011's Glastonbury Festival.

The massive success of 360° helped make up for the album's poor performance. The band played 110 shows, selling 7.2 million tickets and earning $736 million in ticket sales, making the tour the highest-grossing ever in show business history. They finally overtook the previous holders of the record, the Rolling Stones with their A Bigger Bang tour, with a show in São Paulo on 10 April 2011. To mark the occasion that night in Brazil, the band played their first-ever single 'Out of Control'. Bono had written that song on his 18th birthday. He was 51 when the 360° tour ended. What had he, and the band, got left?

> **"The problem was there was no pop song on *No Line on the Horizon*. People say 'Get On Your Boots' was the wrong single, but it's great live. We only figured out how to play it when we were on the road, and it became a much better song."** Bono talking to the author, 2011

OPPOSITE: Bono and Edge play at the last-ever European 360° tour in Rome 2010. Over the course of the two-year tour, they played to more than seven million people.

TOP LEFT: Although massive in scale, the 360° tour also allowed for acoustic, intimate interludes. Here the band perform 'Stuck in a Moment' in Rome 2010.

TOP RIGHT: Adam Clayton and The Edge perform in Gelsenkirchen, Germany in August 2009.

RIGHT: Adam Clayton pictured in New Jersey in 2009 on the 360° tour. Such was the demand for tickets the first time around that the 360° tour had to go back to the US for a second leg two years later.

SONGS OF INNOCENCE

(2014)

Shaken by the response to *No Line on the Horizon*, the band took more than five years coming up with their new album. It was released quietly with just family, friends and 500 million people getting to hear it at the same time.

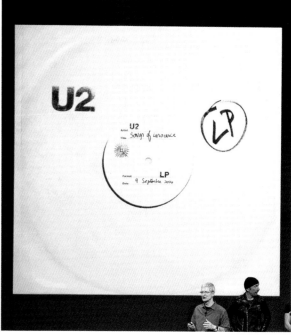

At the Toronto Film Festival in September 2011 for the premiere of *From the Sky Down* (a film about the making of the *Achtung Baby* album), Bono was asked about U2's future in the wake of the disappointing sales of *No Line on the Horizon*. "U2 are now very close to irrelevance," he said with typical candour, adding, "If we don't come up with a very good reason to make a new U2 album, we should just fuck off."

This was how deeply disappointed he was with the reaction to *No Line*.... This was Bono questioning the band's very future and openly wondering if there was a still a place for U2, some 35 years after they had first formed, in a very changed music world.

The fact that it took five-and-a-half years for *Songs of Innocence* (the longest-ever gap between U2 albums) says everything about the band's state of mind while they were recording it. On more than one occasion a release date was announced, only to be postponed as producers came and went and songs got binned, then resurrected, then binned again.

During the recording of a new U2 album, some information normally leaks out about the new music, but this time a veil of secrecy descended. A new single, 'Ordinary Love', was released in November 2013, but this was not from the album; it had been written for the soundtrack of the Nelson Mandela biopic. Then, in February 2014, they released 'Invisible' as a free iTunes download. There was still no album, though.

On the morning of 9 September 2014, during an Apple product launch in Cupertino, California, the band surprised everyone by taking to the stage to announce that *Songs of Innocence* would be made available for free on iTunes. In a move that got headlines and created controversy, U2 had just made their new album instantly available to 500 million iTunes subscribers.

"This is our most personal record ever," said Bono of the new album. The first single, 'The Miracle (of Joey Ramone)' described how seeing a Ramones show in Dublin in 1978 had an evangelical effect on the members of U2.

Another song on the album was about the Dublin street where Bono grew up ('Cedarwood Road') and 'Iris (Hold Me Close)' was about his mother, Iris Hewson. The band were locating the album firmly in their teenage years in Dublin when U2 were playing their first shows.

It was a difficult album to make for the band: going back to the past, they found a lot of dark material. 'Raised by Wolves' is about the worst-ever terrorist outrage in Ireland when car bombs were detonated, leading to the deaths of 33 people. The bombs went off just around the corner from a city centre record shop that Bono used to frequent. 'Sleep Like a Baby Tonight' is a sinister description of a paedophile priest.

Elsewhere they looked at the band's first journeys – 'California (There is No End to Love)' is about U2's first time in Los Angeles while 'This is Where You Can Reach Me Now' is about the four members of U2 going to see the Clash play in Dublin in 1977. As Bono has it, U2 were effectively born the next day as a result of the power and energy of the Clash's show.

The nature of the surprise iTunes launch was typical U2. Here was a band who were openly questioning if they were still relevant; who had struggled to put *Songs of Innocence* together but who then effectively made its release the biggest ever in music history by making it instantly available to 500 million people.

As Bono said from the stage in Cupertino: "From the very beginning U2 have always wanted our music to reach as many people as possible – the clue is in our name. Today is mind-blowing for us as the most personal album we've ever written has just been shared with half a billion people."

As to the long delay behind the album, the singer replied: "We weren't recording one album; we've actually recorded two …"

OPPOSITE, LEFT: U2 play their first new single in five years, 'Invisible', live on *The Tonight Show* in New York, February 2014.

OPPOSITE, RIGHT: The surprise and dramatic release of *Songs of Innocence* at an Apple event in Cupertino, California on 9 September 2014.

RIGHT The band after receiving a Golden Globe award for their song 'Ordinary Love' in January 2014.

BELOW: The band performs 'Ordinary Love' at the Oscars in March 2014.

"We went back to the very beginning to ask ourselves why did we form U2 in the first place and what [does] the band still mean to us today? We went home to Dublin for the answers." Bono

SONGS OF EXPERIENCE (2015)

If the release method of *Songs of Innocence* was a surprise, so was the fact that U2 had a second new album ready to go – and a new digital music format in the pipeline.

By the time the CD of *Songs of Innocence* was released in mid-October 2014, some 30 million people had already downloaded the album free on iTunes. But the physical release sold well – it had two new songs absent from the iTunes download – 'Lucifer's Hands' and 'The Crystal Ballroom' as well as alternate versions of 'The Troubles' and 'Sleep Like a Baby Tonight'.

For Bono, 'The Crystal Ballroom' was the most personal lyric he has ever written. U2 played some of their first-ever gigs in a venue called McGonagles in Dublin. Before it was a music venue it was called the Crystal Ballroom, a place where people used to go for dances. "My mother and father used to dance together in the Crystal Ballroom, so the song is me imagining I'm on the stage of McGonagles with this new band I'm in called U2 and I look out into the audience and I see my mother and father dancing romantically to U2 on the stage," he says of the song.

The sleeve of the *Songs of Innocence* CD – in keeping with the musical theme of the band returning to Dublin in the 1970s – featured a photograph of Larry Mullen embracing his teenage son. It was viewed by the band as the follow-up image to those which featured on their *Boy* and *War* albums.

The album was lauded for the manner in which U2, for the first time, musically told their own story – and for directly acknowledging how two bands in particular, the Ramones and the Clash, were pivotal to the band forming in the first place. Despite being a lyrically retro album, the production (mainly by Danger Mouse) ensured the album had a contemporary sonic sheen.

As a result of all the media noise surrounding iTunes and the physical release of the album, 26 U2 albums (studio albums, live albums, compilations) re-entered the iTunes charts with the highest placing always being for either *The Joshua Tree* or *Achtung Baby*.

It also emerged that the real reason behind the five-and-a-half-year wait for *Songs of Innocence* was because the band were recording two albums simultaneously. A sister album called *Songs of Experience* is due out in 2015. It is believed that as *Songs of Innocence* was all about what

> "Despite everything, the honest truth is that I wish we were a better band, I wish we were a more talented band. We go through excruciating humility these days when songwriting." Bono

happened to U2 in the 1970s, *Songs of Experience* will be about what happened to U2 in the 1980s (Live Aid, *The Joshua Tree*, etc.).

There is also a "secret project" U2 are working on with Apple. The band are working on a new digital music format which will be audio-visual in nature and will be unable to be pirated/illegally downloaded. The hope is that the new format will prove so attractive that people will begin to buy albums again – as opposed to the current practice of just buying two or three songs off an album. The first release on this new format should be the upcoming *Songs of Experience*.

The Innocence + Experience Tour kicks off in Canada in May 2015 and takes in North America and Europe, with all the shows being staged in indoor arenas. When describing the Tour Bono has promised, "We're going to do something live that we've never done before – or anyone's ever done before."

For a band who looked like they were on the ropes over the last few years, the fuss and attention paid to how they released *Songs of Innocence* showed Bono, Edge, Larry and Adam that they do still matter and that they are still capable of surprising and upsetting with their big gestures.

To get to their future, they went back to their past on *Songs of Innocence*.

OPPOSITE: Bono's voice has considerably matured over the years. Thin and overly dramatic in the early days, it now sounds richer and has a more nuanced timbre.

ABOVE: Having had to cancel their Glastonbury 2010 appearance due to Bono recovering from back surgery, the band finally made it to the esteemed festival the following year.

LEFT: The Songs of Innocence tour is planned over two legs, North America and then Europe.

CREDITS

The publishers would like to thank the following sources for their kind permission to reproduce the pictures in this book.

Key: t = Top, b = Bottom, c = Centre, l = Left, r = Right

3. Corbis/Simone Cecchetti, 4. Corbis/Aaron Harris/Retna Ltd., 5. Photoshot/Retna, 6-7. © Patrick Brocklebank, 8. & 9b Getty Images/David Corio/Redferns, 9t. Rex Features/Martyn Goddard, 10. Photoshot/LFI, 11b. Getty Images/David Corio/Michael Ochs Archives, 11tl. Getty Images/David Corio/Redferns, 11tr. & 12. Getty Images/David Corio/Michael Ochs Archives, 13b. Alamy/dpa picture alliance archive, 13tl. Corbis/Henry Ruggeri, 13tr Rex Features/David Pearson, 14r. Getty Images/Clayton Call/Redferns, 14l. Photoshot/LFI, 15b. Getty Images, 15t. Rex Features/Andre Csillag, 16. Getty Images/Stephen Wright/Redferns, 17bl. Corbis, 17br. Mirrorpix, 17t. Rex Features/ITV, 18. Getty Images/Richard E. Aaron/Redferns, 19br. Corbis/Neal Preston, 19bl. Photoshot/Reta, 19t. Getty Images/Ebet Roberts/Redferns, 20. Getty Images/Larry Hulst/Michael Ochs Archives, 21bl. Getty Images/Larry Hulst/Michael Ochs Archives, 21tl. Getty Images/Ebet Roberts/Redferns, 21tr. Getty Images/Steve Haines/The Boston Globe, 21br. Ebet Roberts/Redferns/Getty Images, 22. Getty Images/Peter Noble, 23bl. Corbis/Peter Anderson/The Hell Gate, 23br. Rex Features/Canadian Press, 23tl. Corbis/Henry Ruggeri, 23tr. Photoshot/LFI, 24. Corbis/Neal Preston, 25b. Getty Images/Rob Verhorst, 25tl. Rex Features/Sipa Press, 25tr. Getty Images/Peter Carrette Archive, 26bl. Mirrorpix, 26br. Getty Images/Peter Still/Redferns, 26c. Corbis/Neal Preston, 27b. Getty Images/Phil Dent/Redferns, 27t. Getty Images/Dave Hogan/Hulton Archive, 28. Mirrorpix, 29. Photoshot/LFI, 30. Getty Images/Lex van Rossen/MAI/Redferns, 31b. Corbis/Neal Preston, 31tl. Getty Images/Peter Still/Redferns, 31tr. Corbis/Neal Preston, 32l. Alamy/AF Archive, 32r. Corbis/Neal Preston, 33c. Rex Features/Startracks Photo, 33t. Corbis/David Atlas/Retna Ltd., 34. Corbis/Neal Preston, 35bl. Corbis/Aaron Harris/Retna Ltd., 35br. Getty Images/Peter Noble/Redferns, 35tl. Corbis/Philip Grey/Lebrecht Music & Arts, 35tr. Corbis/Neal Preston, 36b. Getty Images/Rob Verhorst/Redferns, 36t. Getty Images/Ebet Roberts/Redferns, 37b. Getty Images/Rob Verhorst/Redferns, 37t. Getty Images/Bob King/Redferns, 38. Getty Images/Michel Linssen/Redferns, 39l. Getty Image/Michel Linssen/Redferns, 39r. Getty Images/Kevin Cummins, 40. Getty Images/Rob Verhorst/Redferns, 41bl. Getty Images/Michel Linssen/Redferns, 41br. Getty Image/

Brian Brainerd/The Denver Post, 41t. Getty Images/Kevin Cummins, 42. Corbis/Neal Preston, 43bl. Getty Images/David Corio/Michael Ochs Archives, 43tr. Photoshot/LFI, 43br. Corbis/Robb D. Cohen/Retna Ltd., 43tl. Corbis/Neal Preston, 44b. & 44t Corbis/Roger Hutchings/In Pictures, 45b. Corbis/Neal Preston, 45t. Mirrorpix, 46l. Getty Images/Paul Bergen/Redferns, 46r. Getty Images/Bob King/Redferns, 47b. Rex Features/Peter Stone, 47t. Mirrorpix, 48l. Getty Images/John Levy/AFP, 48r. Corbis/Andrew Murray/Sygma, 49b. Getty Images/Paul Bergen/Redferns, 49tl. Getty Images/Tim Mosenfelder, 49tr. Getty Images/Rob Verhost/Redferns, 50c. Getty Images/KMazur/WireImage, 50b. Press Association Images/©Doug Peters/allactiondigital.com, 51. Rex Features/Andy Paradise/The Independent, 52l. Corbis/Guillaume Bonn, 52r. Corbis/Roger Hutchings/In Pictures, 53bl. Rex Features, 53br. Press Association Images/Jonathan Hayward/AP, 53t. Rex Features/Richard Young, 54b. Press Association Images/Bernaut Armangue/AP, 54t. Press Association Images /Pier Paolo Cito/AP, 55b. Getty Images/Bryan Bedder, 55t. Rex Features/Insight-Visual UK, 56. Corbis/Simone Cecchetti, 57b. Alamy Images/Brooke Ismach/ZUMA Press, 57tl. Corbis/Simone Cecchetti, 57tr Alamy/dpa picture alliance archive, 58l. Getty Images/Lloyd Bishop/NBC/NBCU Photo Bank, 58r. Getty Images/Justin Sullivan, 59b. Press Association Images/John Shearer/AP, 59t. Press Association Images/Lionel Hahn/ABACA USA/Empics Entertainment, 60. Rex Features/Startraks Photo, 61b. Corbis/Brad Loper/Dallas Morning News, 61t. Rex Features/Brian Rasic, 62. Alamy Images/AF archive.

Memorabilia: Private Collection

Every effort has been made to acknowledge correctly and contact the source and/or copyright holder of each picture and Carlton Books Limited apologizes for any unintentional errors or omissions which will be corrected in future editions of this book.

ABOVE: An early press photo of the band taken in 1981. The photograph was used on the front cover of issue 1 of the band's own fan magazine.